Praise for
EDGE: Value-Driven Digital Transformation

"This impressive book offers a holistic set of principles and practices that will help enterprises to upgrade their innovative capabilities. With a laser focus on outcomes and value, and relying on a product mindset, lightweight governance, and adaptive leadership, the authors explain how a company can survive and thrive with an agile product portfolio in an increasingly complex environment. This book should be cherished and devoured."

—Jurgen Appelo, author of Management 3.0 *and* Managing for Happiness

"As an entrepreneur who since 2008 has been growing a bootstrapped SaaS company that transforms industrial manufacturers into digital commerce power-houses, I am living on the edge.

"But thanks to *EDGE: Value-Driven Digital Transformation,* I now have a frame-work and vocabulary that I can use to reflect on my journey and visualize my organizational future. More importantly, knowing that the authors' decades of experience and wisdom, encapsulated in EDGE, resonates with mine, I can confidently make this required reading by everyone at Corevist and recommend it to all of our clients who are struggling with their own digital transformations."

—Sam Bayer, CEO, Corevist

"It's refreshing to read a book that goes beyond the 'base camp' of agility. So often we get to Scrum or some framework and then stop. True digital transformation is much more, and this book by Highsmith, Luu, and Robinson captures what every manager needs to know if we want to scale these challenging heights. Highly recommended!"

—Martyn Jones, Managing Director, SoftEd Group, New Zealand

"*EDGE: Value-Driven Digital Transformation* is a valuable book and an indispensable guide to successfully navigating a digital transformation. It's packed with powerfully simple and practical guidance, asking us the questions we need to address. I've found the practical operating-model framework focuses our attention on what really matters (i.e., adopting rapidly enough, developing differentiating capabilities to address emerging opportunities, and creating a sustainable advantage). Equally important are insights of traps that most organizations fall into—and straightforward suggestions of how to prepare.

"Other highlights of value are recognizing paradoxes and practical tips on how to manage conflicting polarities with 'both/and' thinking; how to more effectively and rapidly make decisions informed by empirical data and grounded by well-designed value models; and aligning adaptive strategy to execution.

"Lastly, *EDGE* stresses investing in frequent, effective feedback loops that ensure today's competitive differentiators don't become tomorrow's competitive anchors.

"I believe *EDGE* offers us an indispensable toolkit to navigate life on the 'edge' of uncertainty—and also to create our own, uniquely competitive capability to seize opportunities that are hidden in the emerging chaos: investing for change, working together, and adapting quickly and continuously.

"A 'must' read."

—Pat Reed, former executive roles at Disney, Universal Studios, Gap Inc.;
academic roles at University of Denver, UC Berkeley, and Woodbury University;
entrepreneur and cofounder of iHoriz, Inc.

"With the publication of *EDGE: Value-Driven Digital Transformation*, Jim Highsmith, Linda Luu, and David Robinson have written the book that is precisely what we need to help organizations be successful in the emerging world of the digital future. Agility and adaptiveness are qualities that should be part of all areas of business, but organizations are struggling with the details of how to make the transition. If they invest in the right digital technology, will all their problems be solved, or are there deeper and more pervasive changes that should be made to all of the management systems?

"*EDGE* answers the technology question brilliantly through the concept of tech at the core. It was so well articulated that I sat there slapping my forehead because even ten years at Gartner hadn't made this concept as clear to me as this chapter did. I understood it intuitively before, but I didn't have the right words to explain it, and now I do. This chapter alone would make the whole book worth reading.

"On the management side of the equation, I appreciated the concept of the Lean Value Tree. Organizations struggle with how to clearly define the value of any business decision, especially ones that do NOT lend themselves to a hard ROI. The Lean Value Tree provides a simple and direct approach to determining value, which in turn will help organizations make better investment decisions much more quickly.

"I've been looking for a book to recommend to the company managers I work with, and *EDGE* is exactly the book I had in mind. Thank you."

—*Donna Fitzgerald, Executive Director, NimblePM, Inc.,*
and former Research VP at Gartner

"*EDGE* is an outstanding read for business and technology leaders in search of higher performance, better cultures and a solid set of strategies to ensure your organization succeeds.

"Packed full of clear and concise models and methods to help focus your innovation activities on outcomes and options to get there, *EDGE: Value-Driven Digital Transformation* is the go-to guide for leaders looking to link strategy to how an organization executes on delivery of value, delighting customers, and business results."

—*Barry O'Reilly, business advisor and author of* Unlearn *and* Lean Enterprise

"Agile as a broad business concept has now, finally, gone mainstream. Jim Highsmith was there at the beginning, in the 1990s—one of very few players who created the powerful ideas behind agile. In this new book, these powerful ideas, significantly evolved, are unleashed on the challenge of digital transformation. It's a good fit, and yields potent insights."

—*Robert D. Austin, Professor, Ivey Business School,*
and author of Adventures of an IT Leader

"With our clients, and with our internal initiatives, we need to figure out how to let teams be autonomous, yet focus on common goals. The EDGE framework, and this book that describes it, distills our current best understanding of how to balance that difficult puzzle."

—*Martin Fowler, Chief Scientist, ThoughtWorks*

"Connecting strategy to implementation and modifying an organization's planning process to take advantage of the flexibility software provides is a huge challenge. EDGE provides a framework for addressing that problem. This book is a must-read for anyone working to transform their company to be able to compete in a digital world."

—Gary Gruver, President of Gruver Consulting, previously R&D director
Hewlett-Packard, and VP of QA, Release, and Operations at Macy's.com

EDGE

Value-Driven Digital Transformation

EDGE

Value-Driven Digital Transformation

Jim Highsmith
Linda Luu
David Robinson

✦ Addison-Wesley

Boston • Columbus • New York • San Francisco • Amsterdam • Cape Town
Dubai • London • Madrid • Milan • Munich • Paris • Montreal • Toronto • Delhi • Mexico City
São Paulo • Sydney • Hong Kong • Seoul • Singapore • Taipei • Tokyo

For information about buying this title in bulk quantities, or for special sales opportunities (which may include electronic versions; custom cover designs; and content particular to your business, training goals, marketing focus, or branding interests), please contact our corporate sales department at corpsales@pearsoned.com or (800) 382-3419.

For government sales inquiries, please contact governmentsales@pearsoned.com.

For questions about sales outside the U.S., please contact intlcs@pearson.com.

Visit us on the Web: informit.com/aw

Library of Congress Control Number: 2019944494

Copyright © 2020 Pearson Education, Inc.

Cover image: Yuri Hoyda/Shutterstock

ISBN-13: 978-0-13-526307-5
ISBN-10: 0-13-526307-7

100 2022

Editor-in-Chief
Julie Phifer

Executive Editor
Haze Humbert

Development Editor
Chris Zahn

Managing Editor
Sandra Schroeder

Senior Project Editor
Julie B. Nahil

Copy Editor
Jill Hobbs

Indexer
Cheryl Lenser

Proofreader
Abigail Manheim

Cover Designer
Chuti Prasertsith

Compositor
codeMantra

To Wendie, who has supported me through the
ups and downs of the writing process for the
last 25 years. —J.H.

To my parents Thieu Hue and Thu Thanh, who left
war-torn Vietnam to give us a better future, and my
husband Kevin, for supporting me while I was heavily
pregnant and determined to eat my way through writer's
block. —L.L.

To my mentor and friend Jerry Weinberg, who helped
me become a better consultant and
human being. —D.R.

Contents

Foreword

To thrive in a world of digital disruption and continuous change, we must become agile. How are you becoming agile? I've spent the majority of my career leading and advising businesses on designing new operating and engagement models to drive digital transformation and achieve enterprise Agility through the adoption of fundamentally different ways of working, thinking, and being.

How are you responding to and managing change in your environment? In my most recent executive role in corporate America, I served as a CIO and chief agilist for a *Fortune* 50 company in the financial services industry. The adoption of agile's core values in the software delivery processes at this $35 billion financial services company led to enormous improvements in speed, quality, and productivity—faster, better, cheaper! Yet, several years into this transformation, we reached the edges of scalability and sustainability. It was only then that we began to ask questions: "What else must we transform to better deliver the capabilities our customers need when they need them? Is it possible that agile matters because it enables enterprise agility?"

Are you in the midst of a *transformation* or are you *transforming*? I have discovered that scale is ultimately about creating a lean governance framework that can support networks of empowered teams, relevant measures, and new operating and engagement models. It's a bit more complicated than just standing up more agile teams or adopting the agile mindset.

Enterprise agility is a measure of the ability of the entire organization to respond rapidly to change. As each new opportunity or threat appears, the agile enterprise fluidly remolds itself by deploying its resources to seize the advantage, thereby remaining responsive to the current environment and relevant to the future environment. The agile enterprise recognizes that every aspect of the business has to embrace change. Every aspect of the business has to become agile—from how the CEO sets objectives to how the janitor cleans the floors.

EDGE: Value-Driven Digital Transformation will help you unleash the promise of agile. It will help you build the capabilities to transform. And it will demand that you develop the capacity to embrace and lead change.

Like the "Courageous Executives," the authors of this book are boundless in their thinking, bold in their actions, and passionate about technology. This passion for technology allows them to recognize that for most enterprises in the 21st century, technology is THE business. This is what really separates the EDGE approach. It is a comprehensive operating model with technology at its core, while holistically embracing the four dimensions that make a difference today—speed, adaptability, iterative, and driven by customer value.

Enterprise sustainability demands that organizations are designed for business agility and responsiveness. As the authors astutely point out, the question isn't "Are you able to move fast?" Instead, the question is "Are you able to move fast enough?" Having a clear approach to building the link between strategy and execution—that is, connecting vision to value delivery—will help you transform your organization to adapt fast enough. It will lead you to internal agility—the ability to make significant internal changes fast—which is the defining characteristic of the agile enterprise. To achieve this level of agility, every last corporate internal reflex has to change.

Regardless of where you are on your journey of transforming, know that your digital transformation is ambitious and fraught with great risks and challenges. Also, be comforted in the knowledge that if you embrace change and are willing to ask for help, you can lead your organization to operate in fundamentally different ways.

—*Heidi Musser,*
Executive Vice President and Principal Consultant,
Leading Agile; retired, Vice President and CIO, USAA

Preface

Digital transformation. Transforming to a digital enterprise appeals to senior executives in wide range of industries. They are attempting to stave off the next wave of disruptions that will put their organizations in jeopardy—becoming the latest Blockbuster or Kodak. Research indicates that a significant majority of CEOs aspire to be digital, but a very low percentage think they have been successful. A vast gap lies between strategy and execution—that middle ground that seems so difficult to traverse.

EDGE is not an acronym, but rather an expression that reminds us of the challenges, messiness, and excitement of transforming into a digital enterprise. The title "EDGE" comes from the concept of the "edge of chaos" in complex adaptive systems theory and provides the missing link between digital strategy and value delivery. Transformations require continuous innovation, which in turn requires an edgy culture that challenges the status quo.

EDGE is an operating model that addresses the following issues:

- How people work together when major, fast-paced responses are necessary
- How organizations allocate and monitor investment funds for initiatives based on an organization's vision and goals
- How organizations learn to adapt fast enough to thrive in highly competitive markets

You have seen jokes that begin with an older adult trying to learn some aspect of technology and being referred to a 12-year-old for help. In today's world, you can't afford to be that adult. Executing a digital transformation requires that you view technology from a perspective that we call Tech@ Core, in which everyone, not just the technologists, understands how technology offers both new opportunities that demand new capabilities.

Unfortunately, you can't escape from the status quo using the same measures of success that were used to achieve that status quo. Transformation demands that you change those measures as well. Indeed, one of the most uncomfortable changes for leaders is this change in performance measures. The most profound of these is the change in focus from internal return on investment (ROI) to external customer value, which is fundamentally a change in perspective and your gut-level basis of decision making. Concurrently, the technology measures of success change from cost and efficiency to speed and adaptability.

One of the questions you might ask is "Who is the target audience for EDGE?" The traditional answer might be a CEO, or CIO, or chief digital officer, or CMO, or chief strategy officer. We have a different answer.

Since 1993, ThoughtWorks has partnered with enterprise organizations and leaders around the world to transform their businesses through technology. With thousands of executive relationships and hundreds of transformational journeys, we've identified a unique segment of leaders we call Courageous Executives. Some are breathing new vitality into legacy enterprises, while others are shaking up stale industries with new platforms and business models. They are boundless in their thinking, bold in their actions, and passionate about technology. This is why we believe Courageous Executives are the next major disruptive force in business, creating a powerful competitive advantage through their leadership style.[1]

Whether your job title is CEO, CIO, program manager, or individual contributor, we think the key personal trait for transforming to a digital enterprise is the courage to move forward in the face of uncertainty. Courageous Executives challenge the status quo again and again. Transformation isn't for the faint of heart, and neither is EDGE.

As companies across all industries embrace the changes of our increasingly digital world, we're seeing leaders at the helm of these companies dive deeper into how technology is implemented and how it works. Executives around the globe are learning that a strong grasp of technology matters, and they're finding ways to adapt. A tenacious commitment to embrace technology is what sets apart truly Courageous Executives.[2]

1. Guo, Xiao. "The Next Big Disruption: Courageous Executives." ThoughtWorks, July 20, 2017. https://www.thoughtworks.com/insights/blog/next-big-disruption-courageous-executives.
2. Guo, Xiao. "The Next Big Disruption: Courageous Executives." ThoughtWorks, July 20, 2017. https://www.thoughtworks.com/insights/blog/next-big-disruption-courageous-executives.

Each EDGE chapter focuses, primarily, on either determining which opportunities to invest in or building the capabilities to execute on those investments. Chapters 4–7 address opportunities, whereas Chapters 2 and 8–10 address capabilities.

Moving from a pre-digital technology fitness function of cost/efficiency to a digital one of speed/adaptability requires that enterprises embrace technology in much different ways than in the past. We call this perspective Tech@ Core as technology moves from a support capability to a core capability that everyone—from CEO to clerk—embraces. Chapter 2, Tech@Core, outlines the components you need to think about as part of your digital transformation—from utilizing a technology radar to creating a technology platform.

One of the reasons the agile movement has been vibrant for nearly 20 years has been the influence of the values and principles contained in the Agile Manifesto, which was published in 2001. While there have been efforts to revise these principles, they have remained core to agile's expansion. New agile practices and processes have blossomed over the years, but the core values have endured.

The Manifesto for Agile Software Development

Individuals and interactions over processes and tools
Working software over comprehensive documentation
Customer collaboration over contract negotiation
Responding to change over following a plan[3]

The EDGE principles are extensions of the core agile ones, oriented to the digital transformation of enterprises. They encompass individuals and teams, collaboration, adapting over time, customer value, and concrete results. Chapter 3, EDGE Principles, describes how these principles impact work and working together.

Chapter 4, Building a Value-Driven Portfolio, answers the fundamental question "How should we invest?" We start this process by articulating a clearly understood business vision and then express the strategy to achieve that vision as a Lean Value Tree (LVT) populated with goals, bets, and initiatives. We then describe the necessary processes for attaining this

3. "Manifesto for Agile Software Development." The Agile Manifesto, 2001. http://agile-manifesto.org/.

value-oriented expression of business strategy and how it fundamentally changes the allocation of investments based on customer value rather than internal business benefits.

Although your LVT describes strategy in outcome-oriented terms, you have to determine how to measure those outcomes. That is the subject of Chapter 5, Measuring and Prioritizing Value. Without definitive Measures of Success (MoS), you're left with un-actionable statements for which success or failure is arbitrary. Measures that are defined and articulated correctly become a powerful way to shape work to achieve the desired outcome.

Chapter 6, Building a Product Mindset, covers an important aspect of aligning the whole organization to the delivery of value. The product mindset connects the organizational strategy (LVT) to the teams responsible for delivering the value for the customer. An important part of building this product mindset is applying an experimental approach to the discovery of value and the product skills needed in the organization to connect and align the portfolio teams to delivery teams.

Optimizing for maximum value necessitates combining several different types of work into an integrated backlog for delivery teams so that they can manage the work effectively. Chapter 7, Integrating Strategic and Business as Usual Portfolios, describes how to build that integrated backlog and prioritize different work items using a common measurement—value. One type of work is Business as Usual (BAU), which is often left out when discussing business agility, as the focus of agile development is strategic initiatives and innovation. Based on our experience with clients, typically 80 percent of large enterprises' budgets are spent on BAU, so we see this as an opportunity to maximize value. We describe how to apply EDGE principles to this portion of your portfolio.

Both agile and lean principles guide us to think about value and removing built-up organizational overhead. Techniques like value stream mapping are used to optimize processes and documentation that have ossified and slowed progress. Governance is absolutely necessary—executives and leaders have fiduciary responsibilities—but senseless overhead is unnecessary, as it reduces both speed and adaptability. Chapter 8, Lightweight Governance, describes ways to balance the competing needs of governance and value delivery.

Chapter 9, Autonomous Teams and Collaborative Decision Making, tackles a core EDGE question: "How should we work together?" Working together in a fast-paced, innovative manner requires a special approach to organizing teams and making effective, quick decisions. This chapter delves into the concepts of autonomous teams, collaborative decision making, and aligning organizations to deliver outcome-oriented results. Traditional functional teams suffer in a transformational environment, and even newer "empowered" teams don't go far enough (although "empowered" has been so overused that it's nearly lost its meaning).

Chapter 10, Adaptive Leadership, helps answer two of EDGE's key questions: "How should we work together?" and "How should we adapt fast enough?" Autonomous teams have a great deal of decision-making power, but they still need direction and leadership. But what type of leadership? While traditional management has carried the label "command and control," more recent models have a variety of names—we use "adaptive leadership" to describe this concept. This chapter delves into the leadership behaviors that are necessary for today's Courageous Executives.

Chapter 11, Exploring Your Transformative Future, is the final chapter in this book. It summarizes the key points of the book and looks ahead to what the future may hold.

These principles, practices, and tools have been curated from our work with many global clients, tried and tested, and evolved into a body of knowledge we are excited to share.

Jim Highsmith, Lafayette, Colorado
Linda Luu, San Francisco, California
David Robinson, Evergreen, Colorado
August 2019

Register your copy of *EDGE: Value-Driven Digital Transformation* on the InformIT site for convenient access to updates and/or corrections as they become available. To start the registration process, go to informit.com/register and log in or create an account. Enter the product ISBN (9780135263075) and click Submit. Look on the Registered Products tab for an Access Bonus Content link next to this product, and follow that link to access any available bonus materials. If you would like to be notified of exclusive offers on new editions and updates, please check the box to receive email from us.

Acknowledgments

We are thankful for all the support, opinions, feedback, and contributions from our community of passionate advocates for EDGE. A special thanks to our clients who have pushed and stretched us to go further in defining a new way of working for the industry.

A special shout-out to our ThoughtWorks colleagues, who are the sponsors, brain trust, and contributors to this evolving body of knowledge: Dan McClure, Sriram Narayan, Kylie Castellaw, Gary O'Brien, Rujia Wang, Kraig Parkinson, Natalie Hollier, Joanne Molesky, Chad Wathington, David Whalley, Darren Smith, John Spens, Rebecca Parsons, Jackie Kinsey, Angela Ferguson, Mike Mason, Brandon Byars, Anne Smith, Patti Purcell, and Lauren David.

Thanks to our industry colleagues, some of whom we have worked with for many, many years: Sam Bayer, Heidi Musser, Donna Fitzgerald, Jurgen Appelo, Rob Austin, Barry O'Reilly, Vickie Hall, and Pat Reed. And thanks to the staff at Cannon Mine Coffee, who kept Jim supplied with coffee and pastries through long mornings of writing.

Thanks to graphics designer Shabrin Sultana and production consultant Gareth Morgan.

To the wonderful staff at Pearson who shepherded us through the editing and production process—Haze Humbert, Chris Zahn, and Julie Nahil and freelance copy editor Jill Hobbs.

About the Authors

Jim Highsmith is an Executive Consultant at Thought-Works, Inc. He has 50-plus years' experience as an IT manager, product manager, project manager, consultant, software developer, and storyteller. Jim has been a leader in the agile software development community for the past two decades.

Jim is the author of *Adaptive Leadership: Accelerating Enterprise Agility* (Addison-Wesley, 2014); *Agile Project Management: Creating Innovative Products* (Addison-Wesley, 2009); *Adaptive Software Development: A Collaborative Approach to Managing Complex Systems* (Dorset House, 2000), which won the prestigious Jolt Award; and *Agile Software Development Ecosystems* (Addison-Wesley, 2002). Jim is the recipient of the 2005 international Stevens Award for outstanding contributions to systems development.

Jim is a coauthor of the Agile Manifesto, a founding member of The Agile Alliance, coauthor of the Declaration of Interdependence for project leaders, and cofounder and first president of the Agile Leadership Network. Jim has consulted with IT, product development organizations, and software companies in the United States, Europe, Canada, South Africa, Australia, Brazil, China, Japan, India, and New Zealand.

Linda Luu is a Consultant and Head of Digital Transformation for ThoughtWorks, Inc. North America. She has 20 years' experience building new capabilities in organizations seeking to respond faster to the shifting needs of customers, in the areas of design thinking, big data and analytics, portfolio management, and agile delivery.

In 2010, frustrated by the pace of product development and organizational change at a large bank, Linda left Aussie shores and headed to the United States to learn better ways of working. During this journey, she was fortunate to have the opportunity to work with amazing individuals who pushed the boundaries of how organizations could function both at a macro and team level. This experience made her excited to share the learnings, stories, and many challenges of building organizational responsiveness in today's environment fueled by technological change. Her journey includes working with clients from Australia, North America, Canada, South Africa, and Brazil.

Linda is on the board of Rutgers Big Data Certificate Program. She holds a double degree in commerce (finance) and science (applied math) as well as an MBA from the Australian Graduate School of Management. She is married and a proud mother.

 **David Robinson** is a Principal Consultant at ThoughtWorks, Inc. where he focuses on helping clients drive digital transformation. He is the global leader of the Responsive Organizations offering at ThoughtWorks. David has consulted with large enterprises driving digital transformation in the financial services, transportation, logistics, retail, and entertainment industries across the globe.

David has 30-plus years' experience in information technology as a CIO and other leadership positions. He has grown three start-ups (two wins, one loss), and also spent a few years outside of technology, leading business units. As a recovering executive, David has been focused on building more human organizations by innovating new ways of working that unlock the talent and passion of creative people.

Chapter 1

The Big Picture

Happy the [person] who still can hope
To swim safely in this sea of error
What we need we don't really know
And what we know fulfills no need at all

(Johann Wolfgang von Goethe, Faust Part 1)

Digital enterprise, the Fourth Industrial Revolution, lean enterprise—today's literature teems with exhortations to transform from the old to something new. How are you responding? Do you have your digital strategy in place? How do you plan to "realize" that strategy? Is your enterprise getting incremental outcomes in a world of exponential opportunities? Whether your goals are for your organization to become a digital enterprise, foster widespread innovation, or implement a digital strategy, is your transformation vision thwarted by poor execution?

Klaus Schwab, executive chairman of the World Economic Forum, spared little hyperbole when he said, "We stand on the brink of a technological revolution that will fundamentally alter the way we live, work, and relate to one another. In its scale, scope, and complexity, the transformation will be unlike anything humankind has experienced before."[1] You could think of a digital enterprise (or business) as having made the transformation from the Industrial Age to the Digital Age. An Internet search for "digital enterprise" yields phrases such as "leveraging technology for competitive gain" and "creating

---

1. Schwab, Klaus. "The Fourth Industrial Revolution: What it means, how to respond." World Economic Forum, January 14, 2016. https://www.weforum.org/agenda/2016/01/the-fourth-industrial-revolution-what-it-means-and-how-to-respond/.

new business models." But these definitions are lacking. Leveraging technology and creating new business models are important, but the most critical component is transforming your culture so that it can evolve and adapt quickly. This culture change spans the entire organization, not just your technology divisions. And, this book concentrates on transforming (a verb) rather than transformation (a noun). Most organizations aren't "there"; instead, they are becoming.

> **Definition**
>
> **Digital enterprise**   An enterprise that is transforming itself to meet the challenges of our postindustrial Digital Age, by embracing an adaptive culture, employing technology at its core, and creating new business models.

Enterprises face an ever-growing gap between opportunities and the capability to exploit them. Technological advances generates opportunities, yet enterprises' capabilities—from developing a digital strategy, to portfolio management, to software delivery—often struggle to keep pace. Change, brought about by technology—or indeed other major forces such as globalization or climate change—challenge our ability to adapt rapidly enough. Many organizations suffer from outdated management models, which block their desired strategy from becoming reality. For example, when enterprises have agile teams that deliver features every two weeks but operate within an annual funding cycle, something doesn't jive.

> **The Time Is Now**
>
> Indeed, in a 2017 survey conducted by the MIT Center for Information Systems Research (CISR) of senior leadership from across the globe, 413 senior executives reported that over the next five years their companies may be at risk of losing an average of 28 percent of their revenues because of digital disruption.[2]

2. Weill, Peter, and Stephanie Woerner. "Why Companies Need a New Playbook to Succeed in the Digital Age." *MIT Sloan Management Review* [Blog], June 28, 2018. https://sloanreview.mit.edu/article/why-companies-need-a-new-playbook-to-succeed-in-the-digital-age/.

In complexity theory, there is a concept called the *edge of chaos*.[3] This "edge," lodged between randomness and structure, is where innovation and maximum learning happen. Balancing on this edge requires everyone to work in a messy, exciting realm, where uncertainty is embraced and solutions may be ephemeral. It's not a safe or comfortable place, but it's the place where organizations will invent the future. The big question isn't how to adapt to the rapidly changing environment, but rather how to adapt fast enough. Furthermore, the missing link between digital strategy and execution entails much more than traditional portfolio management. We call this missing link EDGE, because transforming (or becoming) requires continuous innovation and innovation requires an edgy culture that challenges the status quo.

EDGE

EDGE is not an acronym, but an expression that reminds us of the challenges, messiness, and excitement of transforming into a digital enterprise.

Building the capability to evolve and continuously adapt is critical to transforming your organization. Today, the accelerating rate of change is overwhelming most organizations' ability to absorb and respond to changes. You may be fast, but are you fast enough? Can you sustain your ability to adapt over time? Effective digital transformations are not for the timid, but rather for the bold and gritty, hanging out on the edge of chaos. Organizations that think a mobile app or a data lake is enough don't understand that transforming is more about culture, mindset, and embodied principles. This is the hard part. Agile software development has been around for nearly 20 years, yet some organizations still think that implementing a practice or two—iterations, pair programming, daily stand-up meetings—is enough. By clinging to this narrow definition, they fail to embrace the cultural values that are the core of real agility.

---

3. Wheatley, Margaret J. *Leadership and the New Science: Learning about Organizations from an Orderly Universe.* Berrett-Koehler, 1992.

In our work with enterprises in retail, financial, transportation, and other industries, the authors have seen organizations striving to become more responsive, especially to their customers. Organizations are finding that having agile software delivery capabilities is not enough. We worked with a large multinational financial firm recently that was interested in DevOps as a way to increase speed and agility. Our assessment pointed out that the firm was spending an inordinate amount of time planning (not surprising in a big enterprise) and DevOps was not its solution. Rather than focusing on DevOps as a means to an end, the organization needed to rethink its entire value stream to become more agile.

Similarly, organizations transforming themselves into more innovative digital enterprises may find they suffer from strategic misalignment between their business and technology functions. In either case—business agility or strategic alignment—the existing operating model for moving from strategy to execution is flawed. These approaches may be purported to be agile or adaptive, when they are actually merely dressed-up traditional processes that are both heavyweight and bureaucratic. They delude traditional managers into thinking they are making progress—but they don't encourage innovation or risk taking. Figure 1-1 depicts the context of EDGE, an operating model that sits between vision and delivery—the critical link that is often missing.

Figure 1-1
EDGE: an operating model.

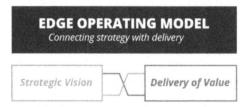

According to a McKinsey study, "IT organizations are asked to innovate at breakneck speed in support of their companies' ambitious digital aspirations (85 percent of respondents want their operating models to be mostly or fully digital, which only 18 percent currently have)."[4] So the vast percentage of organizations have digital aspirations, yet only 18 percent consider themselves successful. Why the disparity? Because there is a big difference between the ambition and knowing how to achieve it. EDGE focuses

4. "Can IT Rise to the Digital Challenge?" McKinsey & Company, October 2018.

on building an enterprise that can respond quickly to customers' needs and emerging technology by defining an operating model that bridges this strategy–delivery gap.

> **Building the Next-Generation Operating Model**
>
> "They have developed next-generation operating models that provide the speed, precision, and flexibility to quickly unlock new sources of value and radically reduce costs. The operating model of the future combines digital technologies and process-improvement capabilities in an integrated, sequenced way to drastically improve customer journeys and internal processes."
>
> —João Dias, David Hamilton, Christopher Paquette, and Rohit Sood, "How to Start Building Your Next-Generation Operating Model," *McKinsey Insights*, March 2017

Exploring EDGE

EDGE's operating model consists of a set of principles and practices that enables your organization to achieve organizational responsiveness.[5] EDGE answers three fundamental questions about your transformation: (1) *How should we work together?*; (2) *How should we invest?*; and (3) *How can we adapt fast enough?* EDGE is designed to sparkle when faced with an enterprise strategy of innovation and transformation. From an operating model perspective, the enterprise needs to embrace EDGE concepts, principles, and practices. From a portfolio management perspective, as discussed in Chapters 5, Measuring and Prioritizing Value, and 7, Integrating Strategic and Business as Usual Portfolios, you can manage an entire IT portfolio while focusing on 10 to 20 percent of the portfolio that is strategic and transformative and, at the same time, integrate Business as Usual (BAU) investments. EDGE is fast, iterative, adaptive, lightweight, and value-driven.

---

5. Although "responsiveness" and "agility" can have slightly different connotations, the authors will use these terms interchangeably.

When you ask the question "How should we work together?", you learn how teams evolve to respond to an environment characterized by an accelerated pace of change. When you ask the question "How should we invest?", you learn to allocate investments and monitor decisions to move faster into our future. When you ask "How can we adapt fast enough?", you learn how to build organizational grit to outpace the competition through continuous learning and adapting fast enough to thrive.

Transforming isn't just about where you invest money and time; equally, or even more, important is how you work together. Agile software delivery teams have learned to plan and deliver in short cycles, measure successful outcomes, experiment with spikes, gather feedback every cycle, and collaborate in autonomous teams. Agile teams "work" differently than traditional software teams do.

EDGE is designed to work in the face of market uncertainty by stressing the importance of adaptability. It helps create the links from your vision to the detailed initiatives you need to undertake. And it's based on making incremental investments, rather than big, upfront funding. EDGE provides support for managing change and transforming your organization to a digital enterprise by changing the mix of investment funds to reflect your new strategy—and by reducing your risk when doing so.

In large enterprises, an annual planning cycle has become customary. Typically, some form of strategic planning process will identify a list of key programs and projects. An estimate of each program and project is then fed into a lengthy budgeting process. In a value-centered world, you replace upfront program funding with incremental funding of the business outcomes to be achieved. You can articulate your business outcomes using Measures of Success (MoS), which describe the value you're willing to pay for. As you demonstrate value to your enterprise and outline the cost to achieve it, you can budget accordingly.

EDGE focuses on the decisions made in an organization. Information—data, spreadsheets, analysis, documentation, surveys and the like—is vital in helping you plot a path to success. But ultimately, information is not enough. To succeed, your decision making has to be informed by experience, judgment, courage, and instinct.

Note that this formula isn't "either/or" but "both/and." It's not analytics or instinct, but a blend of both. Thousands of new opportunities are available to companies every day, and hundreds of possible responses can be made to those opportunities. The great entrepreneurial leaders have the instinct to look at the available, incomplete data and make the correct judgment calls more often than not.

Agility Is Key to Fast Enough

Whether you call it agile, responsive, or adaptive, your entire organization, from executives to delivery staff, needs to embrace a culture of sensing the marketplace and responding to change in an effective way. Scaling agility is more about changing organizational culture than about building bigger things. A number of agile/lean scaling frameworks focus on planning for and building "bigger" things. Unfortunately, they tend to take on the trappings of traditional heavyweight methodologies, including an over-emphasis on documentation and process. What's really needed are frameworks that focus on "better," not "bigger." Scaling agility (as in undertaking large projects) may be a problem, but it's just not as important as the challenges of learning and adapting fast enough. Implementing a digital strategy, or becoming a digital enterprise, must be driven by innovation—in products, in strategy, in technology, in portfolio management, in measures of success, in organization, and more. Transforming to a digital enterprise needs to focus first and foremost on devising better ways of aligning strategy and delivery. Once you are better, then you can focus on bigger. Most (but not all) innovation initiatives aren't huge undertakings, but rather uncertain undertakings.

Scaling agility may be a problem, but it's not as important as the challenges of learning and adapting fast enough.

The authors have been evolving EDGE in our work at ThoughtWorks over a decade. The authors have worked with clients in the telecommunications, financial services, insurance, and retail industries—sectors facing significant disruption in today's Digital Age.

Building Organizational Responsiveness

For the past decade, organizations with software delivery teams have invested heavily in learning agile delivery practices—practices that promise to help the organization eliminate wasted efforts, make better decisions through collaboration and higher-quality output, and move faster. Ultimately, this way of working enables leaders to steer the organization toward delivering more customer value. However, as the previous CEO story shows, organizations scaling agile software delivery practices still lament their inability to realize the promised value of adopting the agile philosophy.

To effectively build organizational responsiveness, your strategy must be broken down into a portfolio of small pieces of value that can be prioritized. Big things take a long time. Small things take a short time. To be responsive and adaptive, you need to work on smaller things, deliver rapidly, and learn quickly from feedback. These small initiatives provide a clearer sense of whether the investments are allocated to the right areas or whether adjustments need to be made. You will need lightweight governance and adaptive leadership to respond to external pressures, improve agility, and focus on value. Moreover, teams must be set up to deliver in an incremental, adaptive way to release often, enabling faster feedback loops with customers and leaders.

Figure 1-2 is a model of how organizations can better pursue new and existing market opportunities and deliver higher value for the investment made. The first component of a responsive enterprise is an executive vision that expresses how the organization intends to prosper in the future.

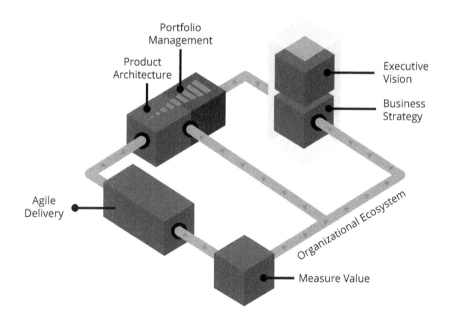

Figure 1-2
Building a responsive organization.

The business strategy states how the business organization intends to achieve the vision expressed as customer outcome goals. Focusing on external customer outcomes and value rather than internal business benefits such as return on investment (ROI) is central to the EDGE message.

The next component and a major focus of EDGE is portfolio management. The investment portfolio is broken down into small pieces. Funding is allocated based on highest value and incrementally allocated until the probability of success is high. This portfolio breakdown enables low-value work to be stopped, with the organization directing its efforts toward the highest-value and limiting work in progress so that teams are focused on one thing at a time. Product architecture translates goals into actionable thin slices of work that agile teams can deliver and measure as incremental successes. Agile delivery builds effective solutions rapidly using practices such as short iterations, design thinking, refactoring, continuous delivery, and evolutionary architecture.

Finally, measurement of value directs teams at all levels to be evaluated on outcomes delivered, rather than what the costs were or whether they met a predetermined delivery date. While costs and schedules are important, they are constraints, not objectives. Measures are broken down to guide teams toward the creation of value.

Toward a Customer-Value Fitness Function

One of the most uncomfortable changes for leaders, especially executives and managers, undergoing digital transformation is the change in performance measures. The most profound of these is the switch from internal ROI to external customer value. While this is a measurement change, it is more fundamentally a change in perspective, a change in your gut-level basis of decision making. It means the first and foremost question an executive leader asks is not "How will this impact our bottom line?" but "How will this impact the value we deliver to our customers?" This change means believing that improving customer value is the key driver that will lead to improved ROI. But ROI isn't the objective; instead, it is a constraint. You need to make a profit to continue delivering customer value. As explained further in Chapter 5, ROI is a business benefit (internal) but not a measure of customer value (external).

The year 2007 was an epic inflection point that has caused turmoil in both the economy and specific enterprises. In his book *Thank You for Being Late*,[6] Thomas Friedman anointed 2007 as the year when multiple technologies came to fruition and kicked "digital" acceleration into high gear. Apple introduced the iPhone, Hadoop ushered in the big data era, GitHub multiplied software development capabilities, Facebook and Twitter expanded the reach and influence of social media, Airbnb showed what small companies could do with these new technologies, the Kindle changed book reading and the publishing business, and Google launched the Android operating system for phones. The confluence of all these technologies enabled new companies, such as Airbnb (which doesn't own a single bed), to become much bigger (more beds than all the major hotel chains—combined). Thus 2007 was the inflection point that separated the pre-digital and digital worlds.

Complexity theory[7] includes a concept called a fitness function.[8] A fitness function summarizes a specific measure to evaluate how close a solution is to achieving a stated goal. In other words, it drives an organism (biology) or an organization (economics) to achieve its purpose—survival and procreation for an organism, thriving and continuation for an organization. As opportunities expand exponentially, you need a process, and a fitness function, to focus investments now and in the future. You need to build capabilities, modern technology platforms, and learning and adaptive practices—all driven by a set of values and principles. As you will see in subsequent chapters, EDGE addresses the challenges of both opportunity and capability. The challenges for enterprises moving from a pre-digital to a digital world are two-fold. First, you must change your fitness function. Second, you must leverage resources to make that change quickly. Both of these will challenge the best organizations.

---

6. Friedman, Thomas L. *Thank You for Being Late: An Optimist's Guide to Thriving in the Age of Accelerations*. New York: Farrar, Straus and Giroux, 2016.
7. For background in complexity theory, see Holland, John H. *Emergence: From Chaos to Order*. Reading, MA: Addison-Wesley, 1989.
8. A related concept in complexity theory is that of a fitness landscape—think of a mountain range—that describes all the various possibilities for entities (agents) that are trying to move up to a higher value of their fitness function.

"It is not the strongest of the species that survives, nor the most intelligent that survives. It is the one that is the most adaptable to change."

—Charles Darwin, English naturalist

The fitness functions or business goals (Table 1-1) from pre-digital to digital times have changed from focusing on ROI to focusing on customer value. In a world characterized by greater certainty, ROI goals made sense. In today's world filled with growing uncertainty, they don't. In a post-2007 world, customer value works better. The switch from an ROI goal to a customer value goal is profound, and experience has shown the transition to be very difficult. Furthermore, trying to change the technology fitness function without changing the business fitness function is a lost cause, as many organizations have discovered to their great chagrin.

Table 1-1
Changing Fitness Functions

Fitness Function	Pre-Digital	Digital
Business	Return on investment	Customer value
Technology	Cost/efficiency	Speed/adaptability

Critics may say that customer value is too intangible, that ROI is a tangible measure and therefore better. In the book *How Leaders Build Value*,[9] the authors suggest that 85 percent of a company's market capitalization can be attributed to intangible factors such as leadership, culture, and patents. Investors look at the stream of earnings volatility over time to determine a price they will buy at (which drives market capitalization), and intangibles drive that stream—you just have to look at an intangible like Steve Jobs's leadership at Apple to prove the point. Look at the market capitalization of high-tech firms today versus that of traditional firms—how much of their capitalization is due to intangible factors?

9. Irich, Dave, and Norm Smallwood. *How Leaders Build Value: Using People, Organization, and Other Intangibles to Get Bottom-Line Results.* Hoboken, NJ: Wiley, 2006.

Changing Competitive Environments

One thing we have learned from clients is that often processes, practices, or software systems that have been competitive differentiators become competitive anchors. A large financial company based its success on a core software application that agents used when working with clients and prospects. The application was so complex that the company couldn't expect customers to use it as they contemplated moving to a customer interactive system. Making the switch from an internal agent–oriented system to an Internet-based self-service system meant a fundamental change in the firm's business model. What had been its key differentiator in the market became an anchor to change.

Given the turbulence and uncertainty of today's business environment, picking the right measures of customer value and other intangible factors can be daunting. Nevertheless, one of the key capabilities required is the ability to discover and capitalize on the opportunities that this turbulence creates. A company's ability to take advantage of opportunities requires a number of intangible factors critical to sustaining a flow of earnings. Customer value has both tangible (financial) and intangible components, intangibles are critical to long-term success, and the ability to deliver customer value is a critical capability for most companies.

Table 1-1 outlines the pre-digital and digital fitness functions. Industrial-era competitive advantage came from efficiency, optimization, and economies of scale. In the digital era, success comes from capabilities such as innovation, adaptability, personalization, customization, and quick response. In Table 1-1, business and technology are functional areas, not organizations. Business and technology organizations don't have separate fitness functions; instead, both have customer value as a primary fitness function. If you are in the technology "organization," your primary fitness function is customer value and your secondary fitness function is speed/adaptability.

Looking at the table, you should not conclude that ROI and cost/efficiency are now unimportant—in fact, they are very important. They are not the primary drivers, but they are secondary, but still critical measures. You might think of customer value and speed/adaptability as the primary objectives and ROI and cost/efficiency as guardrails (constraints).

At the same time the business fitness functions have been transitioning, the technology transition has been moving from cost and efficiency to speed and adaptability (of course, customer value is everyone's primary fitness function). This transition is illustrated by an article and a book published 10 years apart. In 2003, Nicholas Carr wrote a controversial article in the *Harvard Business Review* titled "IT Doesn't Matter,"[10] which argued that IT had become a commodity and, therefore, could not contribute to sustainable competitive advantage. This article emphasized the focus on cost reduction, as it is the path to success for a commodity product. IT organizations were constantly admonished to reduce costs, a focal point that caused ballooning technical debt further impeding their digital transformation.

Ten years later, Rita McGrath,[11] professor at Columbia Business School, wrote that in today's fast-paced, uncertain world, sustainable competitive advantage itself was no more, being replaced by transient competitive advantage in which learning and adapting quickly was the ticket to success. In Carr's world, IT should be governed by cost considerations. In McGrath's world, responsiveness and customer value should drive IT.

The 2007 technological inflection point has exacerbated the difference between the rate of opportunity growth and the building of capabilities to take advantage of those opportunities. Opportunities are expanding so fast that you need ways to accelerate your ability to identify which opportunities to invest in and whether your organization has capabilities necessary to deliver on those investments. In short, you need more leverage. Leverage amplifies the results from a given set of inputs. Many enterprises are facing an existential crisis. They see a world of opportunities, but lack the capability to take advantage. They're being outpaced and outfought by the competi-

10. Carr, Nicholas G. "IT Doesn't Matter." *Harvard Business Review*, May 1, 2003. https://hbr.org/2003/05/it-doesnt-matter.
11. McGrath, Rita Gunther, and Alex Gourlay. *The End of Competitive Advantage: How to Keep Your Strategy Moving as Fast as Your Busines*s. Boston, MA: Harvard Business Review Press, 2013.

tion. This growing opportunity–capability gap has become a critical issue for executive leadership (Figure 1-3). Overcoming this gap requires innovative thinking and putting tech at your business's core, from strategy to delivery.

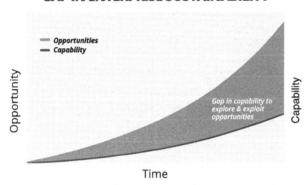

GAP IN ENTERPRISE SUSTAINABILITY

Opportunity

- - - Opportunities
— Capability

Gap in capability to explore & exploit opportunities

Capability

Time

Figure 1-3
The widening gap between opportunities and the capability to explore or exploit these opportunities.

Switching fitness functions, either business or technology, has proved much more difficult than expected. When all of your processes, practices, accounting methods, and performance measures are ROI-driven, and have been for many years, switching to a customer value focus requires courageous business leaders. Similarly, switching IT from a cost/efficiency driver to one of speed/adaptability requires courageous technology leaders.

Making it to, and over, the next horizon requires that you be faster than the competition, adaptable enough, iterative, and driven by customer value. Being faster than the competition requires knowing the competition, which you often don't until late in the game. Being adaptable enough includes understanding the rate of change in your market segments and what new market segments might impact yours. Being iterative means getting quick feedback to steer toward your ultimate vision. Having a customer-value focus means looking from the outside in, rather than the other way around.

A product (or service) is what you deliver to a customer to capitalize on an opportunity. A capability is how you build the what. You need specific strategies and plans for both product and capabilities to narrow the opportunity–capability gap. Your capability development plans should answer the question, "Can we make what we want to sell—*in the future?*" In this book the authors will address these two aspects: capitalizing on opportunities in the form of delivering customer value by investing wisely and increasing the speed of building the capabilities (especially technological capability) necessary to achieve that.

The core question is how you make this fitness function transition fast enough to close the gap between opportunities and capabilities. How do you gain leverage, multiplying your capabilities? How do you combine components, both technological and intellectual, in a way that significantly increases your capabilities?

Customer value is key to the present. Adaptability is key to the future. When ROI and efficiency dominated the fitness function, adaptability suffered. In the technology realm, for example, IT software assets accumulated technical debt that severely impacted future development. Time and time again, when priority decisions were made the emphasis was on schedule and cost, not value and adaptability. Over time, software assets degraded to the point that many organizations' abilities to become digital enterprises were severely compromised.

It's Not Easy, Just Imperative

"In a new McKinsey Global Survey on digital transformations, more than eight in ten respondents say their organizations have undertaken such efforts in the last five years."

"Only 16 percent of respondents say their organizations' digital transformations have successfully improved performance and also equipped them to sustain change in the long term."

—McKinsey & Company, "Unlocking Success in Digital Transformations," October 2018

As noted in the 2018 McKinsey article, even digitally savvy industries have only a 26 percent success rate, versus a success rate of 4 to 11 percent for traditional industries. We will never say such a transition is easy; the McKinsey data and our personal experience agree that it's not. The changes outlined in this book cover the gamut from measuring success, to leadership style, to capability building, to investment strategies. You will find different practices or ideas to plug into your organization's approach to transforming.

But in some way or another, your efforts need to cover all the bases we've mentioned—from how teams work to make collaborative decisions to embracing technology. So it's hard. What other choice do you have?

There is a telling phrase in the second quote from the McKinsey article: "and also equipped them to sustain change in the long term." Only 16 percent of the respondents to McKinsey's survey reported success at improving performance and sustaining it. Another 7 percent improved performance, but could not sustain it. One key question addressed in this book is "How can we adapt fast enough?"—a question that is related to sustainability. Fast enough isn't a one-time goal, but one that continues into the future. Transformation is not a one-shot deal as many organizational changes are—it will be a continuing process of evolution. Sustainability makes the transformation process even harder.

From the very outset, the agile movement was about mindset much more than practices. The same is true for EDGE. For example, Chapter 4, Building a Value-Driven Portfolio, is about building a Lean Value Tree and developing Measures of Success. Similar practices to these have been used by managers for many years. However, building these artifacts using a particular mindset—one that thinks of customer value first, that values short iterations and quick feedback, that is more comfortable with evolving rather than planning solutions, that revels in being part of an autonomous team—makes a huge difference in how these practices are implemented. In turn, a key goal of this book is to provide you with a contextual framework to not only adopt for yourself but also to use to help change the mindset of your colleagues. If you don't change your mindset, none of these practices will help achieve the digital transformation you seek.

Final Thoughts

The concepts and models introduced in this chapter are intended to help you navigate and put into context the specific practices introduced throughout the book. As you progress in your reading, keep the following points in mind:

- EDGE is an operating model that connects strategy to delivery. It does not cover how to *do* either strategy or delivery.

- The relentless focus is on delivering customer value. Customer value is an outcome rather than an output. For example, the number of features that a delivery team produces is an output, whereas the value that they deliver is an outcome.
- Today's world is awash with opportunities. You must first determine which opportunities you wish to pursue. Then, you must build the capabilities necessary to capitalize on those opportunities. Opportunities and capabilities are both driven by outcomes, but they are different types of outcomes.
- If you want your enterprise to be responsive (agile, adaptive), then you have to change your measures of success at the highest level—you must modify your fitness functions to encourage the responsiveness you desire.
- Fundamental change must be driven by courageous executives who are supported by courageous leaders at all levels.
- EDGE is not prescriptive, but adaptive. Every implementation of EDGE will be different, including yours. The core that will hold your version of EDGE together is the principles.
- Building capabilities for the future, from technical ones to portfolio prioritization, is critical for determining what you want to accomplish and how you intend to get there.
- The products that emerge from delivery teams should be driven by the Lean Value Tree: Goals, Bets, and Initiatives. The product blueprints ensure that the teams are looking ahead to understand the product evolution. The technology component ensures that the technology strategy and platform support the Lean Value Tree and the product blueprint.

Whether you are setting high-level goals or building capabilities or delivering a small increment of a product, the fundamental approach you need can be summarized in two simple words: **Envision–Explore**. These two words contrast with traditional approaches that can be characterized by two other words: **Plan–Do**. You can't plan your way into the future—you need to explore. Planning raises the specter of determinism: Just plan well enough, and then just do what you planned. In times of uncertainty and with an accelerated pace of change, our traditional reliance on planning won't work. It's not that we don't plan—we do. In fact, much of this book is about planning. We just don't believe our plans will survive reality. We don't waste time doing detailed plans that change constantly. We spend more time trying to envision the future, whether of our organization or of our detailed initiatives. You can't plan away uncertainty; instead, you have to learn it away. You have to try five things in parallel, in short experiments, to find the one that seems to work and is worth carrying forward. This Envision–Explore mindset needs to permeate your organization if it is to be successful at digital transformation.

As you move into the Fourth Industrial Revolution, where uncertainty reigns and the need for speed and innovation is the dominating force, portfolio and program management must be much more responsive than they have been in the past. Moreover, they must be incorporated into a broader operating model. The path to a digital enterprise lies in being innovative, fast, value centered, and adaptive—not in returning to the structure and process of earlier times.

Chapter 2

Tech@Core

The challenges of becoming digital are two-fold, as introduced in Chapter 1, The Big Picture. The second of these challenges is leveraging your resources to make that change quickly—that is, building and deploying the right capabilities.

In transforming your organization, you have to change how you view technology. Think about Amazon, Google, Netflix, or any of a number of high-tech companies. Technology doesn't "assist" their business—technology *is* their business. You might not compete directly with these high-tech companies, but you are (or will be) competing with companies that are as technically savvy. Tech marketing guru Geoffrey Moore made an observation a number of years ago that a "bank was just a computer with a marketing department." More recently John Chambers, executive chairman of Cisco Systems, said, "At least 40% of all businesses will die in the next 10 years … if they don't figure out how to change their entire company to accommodate new technologies."[1]

Over the years, prognosticators have made statements like these:

- The market for computers will not be more than a dozen units.
- Minicomputers will never replace mainframes.
- Personal computers will never replace minicomputers.
- The Internet will always be for geeks.
- Cell phones are just a niche market.
- Digital cameras will never replace film.
- The smartphone market will be small because of the cost.
- Agile is OK for small, online projects, but it will never replace waterfall processes, "not while I am here."

1. Keynote address, BoxWorks 2015 Conference.

How many companies have gone down in flames as a result of believing these prognostications? Who is next? Don't let it be your organization. As George Westerman, principal research scientist with the MIT Sloan Initiative on the Digital Economy, says, "When digital transformation is done right, it's like a caterpillar turning into a butterfly, but when done wrong, all you have is a really fast caterpillar."

A Digital Enterprise: Technology at the Core

Tech@Core is a concept given birth in this century and coming to the fore as technological opportunities are overwhelming organizations of all kinds. Tech@Core is a simple idea with a complex implementation that is as much cultural as technological. The two key questions to answer are: "What is Tech@Core?" and "Why is it relevant to EDGE?"

> *Tech@Core means that technology is your business—*
> *no matter what your business.*

Tech@Core may best be defined by looking at a little history. Figure 2-1 illustrates the evolution of integration between business and tech, from IT having a supporting role to tech being core to your business.[2]

Figure 2-1
Tech is now, more than ever, a strategic differentiator.

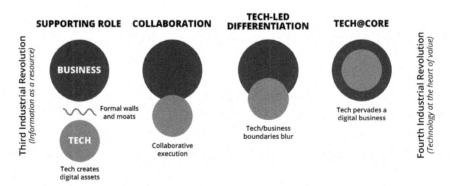

2. This diagram is used by ThoughtWorks staff to illustrate the transition to Tech@Core.

The Evolution of Tech@Core

In the beginning (circa 1970s), business and tech were separated by formality. Tech was the keeper of dark "secrets," and business people didn't want to become involved. The business people might sit still for a few requirements-gathering interviews, but then didn't want to be bothered with all the techie stuff. On the flip side, tech was new and exciting, and the tech people were content to retire to their cubbyholes to perform their magic. They were excited about the technology, but not so much about business issues. This was the era in which many basic business functions—accounting, payroll, inventory control—were first automated. Tech enjoyed success in this phase, in what was deemed a "supporting role," in great part because tech was fairly simple and the business applications being developed had well-known specifications.

The second phase of this history is labeled the "collaboration" phase. As business requirements grew and became more complex, tech became more complex as well. In turn, communications between business and tech needed to improve. During this period, formality in terms of sequential (or waterfall) development life cycles was introduced. This gave rise to the role of systems analysts (who later evolved to become business analysts), who tried to develop a more collaborative relationship with business application users. The systems analysts had more business process knowledge and involved business users during the requirements phase, but the business people still shied away from understanding the technology. Tech to them was still a big black box.

As technology evolved that enabled more business connectivity (online and then early Internet-based applications), tech/business boundaries began to blur and the third era of tech-led differentiation began. This era led to early tech disruptions, such as occurred in the financial industry with the rise of online brokerage firms like Charles Schwab. Tech began to move from the back office (accounting) to the front office (customer interaction). The technology was more complex and the application requirements more nebulous, leading to the need for closer collaboration between tech and business and better understanding of each other's knowledge arenas.

But as business people became more tech savvy, their new knowledge made things both better and worse. Matters became better as business people began to understand how tech could make a real impact, but became worse because their tech knowledge was typically shallow. Frustrated by the slow pace of tech development, some business people began to create their own "shadow IT"—that is, they built their own applications using spreadsheets and other user-oriented tools on their personal computers, hired consultants directly without IT involvement, or purchased a SaaS application with their credit cards. They increasingly made ill-informed comments: "I can build a spreadsheet application in a week. Why does it take IT 9 months?" And they were serious. The fact that these spreadsheet apps often addressed only a single person's needs, didn't scale, weren't maintainable, and created a security risk never crossed the users' minds—their knowledge was shallow.

However, many of these apps delivered real value. From IT's perspective, this problem was exacerbated by legacy system technical debt (still an issue) that had been building for years and acted (and continues to act) as an anchor on software development. In addition, the ballooning need for interactive systems split many IT organizations into legacy system and interactive system groups. Because the interactive technology was more complex and the requirements even fuzzier, development processes (waterfall versus agile) in the two IT factions evolved in different ways, causing increasing friction.

The fourth era, labeled Tech@Core, moves toward greater integration of the business and IT arenas. Among the factors that differentiate Tech@Core from the preceding phases are the following:

- Leaders[3] understand the critical nature of tech to their business and are increasingly tech savvy (many are younger and never worked in the pre-Internet world).
- Leaders depend on technology to create innovative customer journeys.
- Customer value replaces cost as the primary performance measure (fitness function).

---

3. We will use the term *leader* for all types of leaders: executives, managers, and teams for both business and technical arms of the organization.

- Speed and adaptability replace cost and efficiency as technology drivers.
- Tech knowledge and experience are continuously evolving.
- Leaders promote fast, frequent experimentation and learning, while maintaining the discipline to select and evaluate the right experiments.
- Reducing cycle time maximizes the value from learning.

ThoughtWorks' 2017 report on courageous executives supports the first bullet point: "Courageous executives know grasping the ins and outs of technology matters: 54% have developed a deep understanding of technology and a remarkable 57% have written code."[4]

The notion of "technology as the core of business strategy" is spreading to the next frontier. Businesses whose products are easily digitized (finance, media, telecommunications) and businesses that were about distribution and intermediaries (travel agencies and e-commerce) are already there. Now it is the turn of businesses that consider manufacturing to be a core competency (automotive), industries where knowledge has traditionally been the core capability (medicine, pharma, legal, research), and industries that are highly regulated (taxi, government, utilities).

Figure 2-1 suggests that the transition from tech in a supporting role to Tech@Core followed a linear progression. That's not really the case. While large, long-term businesses will have portions of their technology assets in each of these categories, their overall approach to tech is the key. The term "core" is not used lightly here. It goes beyond technology being important or critical to your business to indicate that technology *is* your business. Unless this attitude truly permeates your business, whether your organization is a pure tech company like Google or one that manufactures garden plows, your chances of surviving the digital revolution are slim. But the evolutionary phases are also cumulative. Larger, long-running enterprises will likely have systems, people, processes, tools, and technologies in the latter three of these phases.

---

4. Guo, Xiao. "The Next Big Disruption: Courageous Executives." ThoughtWorks, July 20, 2017. https://www.thoughtworks.com/insights/blog/next-big-disruption-courageous-executives.

The second question asked at the beginning of this chapter was "Why is Tech@Core relevant to EDGE?" At its essence, Tech@Core is changing your fundamental view of technology from thinking about it as supporting your business to thinking about it as an integral, inseparable component of your business. At one level, the question seems almost irrelevant, given that we're talking about transforming to a digital enterprise that embodies technology. However, we can't make the point strongly enough that this chapter is not for the technical staff, but rather for both IT and business leaders. Your leaders and executives need to internalize the concept that technology no longer supports your business, but rather is your business. Understanding the components of Tech@Core should help with this internalization.

You may think that the phrase "technology is your business" overstates the case—and maybe so. But we need to overstate the case to state the case. No aspect of a business—from product development to manufacturing—survives without the other components. But the future—for many, many businesses—lies in becoming digital. And becoming digital is everyone's job. The key question is, How do you accomplish this?

Developing a Technology Strategy

If your vision is to become a highly competitive digital enterprise in the next three to five years, then you need a technology strategy that contains the components required to make that transition. Furthermore, you can't make the transition with a "more of the same" technology strategy and execution. A couple of cautions apply here. First, approach this task with your agile hat on. Agilists plan and they document, but they certainly don't turn the process into a lengthy, document-centric one. Fast feedback, iteration, and learning are just as important here as in product development. Second, communicate and collaborate first and document second (or third).

Jim once worked with a telecom firm in the east. Its architects had developed extensive documentation full of diagrams and standards. When Jim talked to the development staff, he asked if they understood the architecture. "Nope," they said, "the documents don't make much sense to us."

When Jim talked to the architecture staff about how they communicated in person in the past or how they planned to do so in the future, their response was "We don't have time to meet with them. We have to work on analysis and documentation." Don't fall into this trap: Everyone needs to keep an agile hat on, no matter what his or her task.

To broaden and strengthen your technology capabilities, you need to take the following steps:

- Shift your technology fitness function to speed and adaptability.
- Accelerate your technology edge over competitors.
- Maintain awareness and take advantage of technology shifts and trends.
- Develop a digital technology platform strategy.
- Reduce technical debt to increase speed and adaptability.
- Get your key tech staff involved and constantly improving their capabilities.

Embracing Tech@Core means keeping up with technology—a daunting task today. Which technologies do you monitor? Which ones do you experiment with? Which ones do you set aside? Which ones do you embrace? Fifteen years ago, few people anticipated the impact of cloud computing or big data or social media. At that time, a software tech stack (layers of programs to accomplish specific tasks) might have 5 components. Today, these stacks often exceed 15 components, further complicating your tech strategy to keep ahead.[5] How do you monitor what might appear next on the technological horizon?

Embracing a tech strategy should not be undertaken lightly. However, it is clear that if your organization wants to become a digital enterprise and maintain a competitive edge, then embracing tech is a necessity. Do you really have a choice? Where are the bookstores, record stores, and film cameras of yesteryear? Why have so many retail stores closed or gone bankrupt (for example, Toys-R-Us)? If you still view digital technology as something the IT department is responsible for, you might as well start the countdown to your organization's demise.

5. Highsmith, Jim, Mike Mason, Neal Ford. *The Implications of Tech Stack Complexity for Executives.* ThoughtWorks Insights, December 2015.

Note

Older organizations whose IT assets were not built to support a digital enterprise are often in a state that lies somewhere between abysmal and laughable. Years and years of treating IT as a cost center rather than a value center have resulted in mountains of technical and organizational debt. This debt serves as a drag on delivery speed, adaptability, and value generation. Although strategies to evolve out of this situation do exist, their implementation requires a thoughtful plan and persistence.

A tech capability strategy should be derived from your enterprise vision and goals. Your vision to increase tech capability might be as broad as "integrate technology into every aspect of our business" or as specific as "transform our product-line technology capability to adapt quickly to industry changes." Clear capability goals also require new measures of success (measures of adaptability and speed): You can't expect a different outcome if you keep old measurements.

As stated in Chapter 1, becoming a digital enterprise requires a change in fitness function, a change in the highest level of how you measure success in your organization. In the pre-digital world, the business fitness function tended to be return on investment (ROI). In the digital world, it is customer value. For technology, the fitness function is also undergoing a big change—from cost and efficiency to speed and adaptability. Make no mistake: These changes in fitness functions are monumental, but absolutely necessary to make the transition.

In the technology realm, speed and adaptability might appear to be conflicting goals. In some instances, they may require a tradeoff, but to a great extent they reinforce each other. Part of the problem lies in the existence of a project culture rather than a product culture. In a project culture, teams strive to deliver features based on a traditional schedule, scope, and cost objectives, knowing that long-term maintenance will be left to another team. This culture drives development staff to cut corners, to limit testing, and to take other shortcuts that negatively impact adaptability. The project culture also encourages leaders to define up front a set of expected features, and success is perceived as the number of features delivered within the specified time frame and budget, rather than in terms of how extendable and adaptable the product is. That said, there will always be projects, especially during your transition to a product mindset. Likewise, problems can also arise in a product culture,[6] but it has a better chance of delivering continuous value over time.

The technical debt chart (see Figure 2-4 later in this chapter) shows that software degrades over time in an exponentially increasing fashion. You need to adopt strategies first to avoid this degradation, and then to bring the curve down for existing applications. The key to pursuing speed and adaptability at the same time is to view software technology as a continuously evolving asset, instead of something that is built once and then maintained. Adding quality and cycle time to the mix of success measures helps ensure that new features of technology assets can be added over a long period of time.

In developing your tech strategy, you also need to analyze three types of time horizons—continuing the existing business, growing new opportunities, and experimenting with future opportunities.[7] Time frames for these three horizons will vary from business to business, but a rough starting point might be one to two years, three to five years, and more than five years. These horizons will help guide investment decisions. Near-term objectives will probably garner more investment, and far horizons less, but all three horizons should be included in every budget cycle. These different horizons do need to be in different portfolios because they should have different measures of success, especially to ensure future endeavors receive enough funding.

As long as your enterprise operates on a ROI fitness function, transforming it into a digital enterprise will be a nearly impossible quest. Finding out how to balance speed and adaptability, and how to foster both at the same time, will be a critical portion of your technology strategy. Finally, it is essential to get the technology part of your transformation right.

6. Chapter 6, Building a Product Mindset, on developing a product mindset, further describes the differences between a product and project culture.
7. For more information, see McKinsey and Company's three-horizons model.

Seismic Shifts and Trends

Understanding seismic shifts and trends[8] will help you develop an effective technology strategy. They are lenses through which you can view the changing business and technology landscape. You can also think of these shifts as a storyline that plays out over time as different aspects of the story unfold. Shifts also provide us with a container to organize trends that are more specific and detailed. For example, starting in the early 2000s, the "agile" wave ushered in a seismic shift in software development. Agile included specific trends such as Scrum, XP, test-first, and continuous integration. Examples from the 1990s include object-oriented (OO) programming and SmallTalk. OO programming was a major shift at the time and became a standard "method" of programming over time. SmallTalk, by contrast, was a specific language that attracted acolytes for a time but didn't survive the introduction of other OO languages.

Shifts and trends evolve together. Sometimes a series of trends indicate a seismic shift, sometimes shifts begin to emerge independently, and some trends don't fall within a specific shift.

The organizations with successful [digital] transformations are likelier than others to use more sophisticated technologies such as artificial intelligence, the Internet of Things, and advanced neural machine-learning techniques.[9]

For each shift and trend, you need to acquire, analyze, and formulate a variety of data:

- Signals: What are you seeing that is indicative of this shift?
- Business impact: How might this shift affect your enterprise?
- Horizon—what is the time horizon for the trends within this shift?
- Urgency: How urgently do you need to react to this trend?

---

8. The material in this section was excerpted and revised from ThoughtWorks' presentations and articles that we use internally and to advise clients.
9. McKinsey & Company. "Unlocking Success in Digital Transformations." October 2018.

- Technical impact: What capabilities will you need to implement your strategies?
- Actionable advice: What advice will you offer your enterprise on how to approach and use these shifts and trends?

An example is helping in understanding this shift/trend framework. The shift described as "Evolving Interactions" entails advancing from screen-and-keyboard to true "multimodal" interactions—that is, moving between speech, gesture, tactile, and mixed reality interfaces. Rapid evolution of these technologies and the "cellphoneization" of virtual reality (VR)/augmented reality (AR) will give us both better realism and cheaper hardware.

The following signals indicate that this shift is taking place:

- Increased accuracy of voice recognition technology
- More speech platforms (Amazon Alexa, Bing Speech, Google Cloud Speech API)
- Reduced costs for VR/AR headsets
- Emergence of a dominant AR/VR player in the market, as the trend becomes real

The "Evolving Interactions" trend may potentially impact your business in the following ways:

- Growing consumer expectation of chat bots, intelligent agents, and "live" interactions
- Major bot/speech/artificial intelligence (AI) players—Apple, Google, Facebook, Amazon, Microsoft—that heavily disrupt digital engagement strategies
- Potential disintermediation of end-user suppliers given access through Siri/Alexa
- Delivery of functionality becomes more complicated than ever—exploding number of channels, Omni channel++

This trend may also impact on your technical capabilities:

- Skills and capabilities (but you might not need to know it all—how to buy instead of how to build)

- Can you possibly hire enough designers?
- Design capabilities evolve: you need multimodal interactions, and interaction design in space instead of on a screen
- Speech and image recognition technology

Actionable advice consists of more granular advice than the business impact statements just presented. Examples of advice for AR/VR/machine learning (ML) and machine learning/AI might be:

AR likely has a bigger impact than VR. Understand if this is true for your business, the likely business impacts of these technologies, and get involved in the global community.

Ensure prerequisite capabilities are in place, including data engineering and management of large data sets. Then consider how ML and AI can be applied in business contexts.

One approach we have found useful in looking at tech trends is to plot each trend on a chart like Figure 2-2, with the time horizon on one axis and the urgency of action on the other axis. In this chart, the urgency horizons are named a little differently than those on McKinsey and Company's three-horizons model, as they indicate the visibility of the technology rather than an investment category. Investment categories need to include your time horizon as well as other factors. Often, the fuzzy future gets sacrificed to the more tangible needs of the present. Determining the balance between investing in the now, the near future, and the far-off horizon needs to be accomplished at the executive level, and having a visual aid like Figure 2-2 can assist in that process.

Seismic shifts and tech trends could significantly alter your business plans. If you can understand what these shifts and trends are, early in their life cycle, you may be able to get out in front of them and use them to your competitive advantage. Then again, you might get too far out in front and suffer the consequences. Sometimes you cross over from the leading edge to the bleeding edge—Google glasses spring to mind as an example. Every organization needs to figure out just how far to push into its technology crystal ball gazing, trying to balance going far enough with going too far. The faster the pace, the more critical the timing and use of experimental practices become.

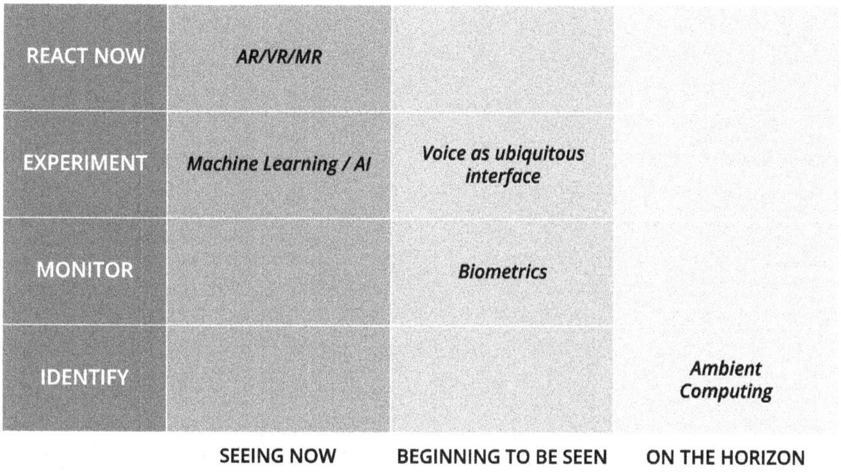

	SEEING NOW	BEGINNING TO BE SEEN	ON THE HORIZON
REACT NOW	AR/VR/MR		
EXPERIMENT	Machine Learning / AI	Voice as ubiquitous interface	
MONITOR		Biometrics	
IDENTIFY			Ambient Computing

Figure 2-2
Projection of seismic shifts over three time horizons.

Creating a Tech Radar

A tech radar is a tool to foster discussions about technology trends and how they might benefit your enterprise. Figure 2-3 shows a sample quadrant of a recent ThoughtWorks radar.[10] This radar focuses on software technology, but depending on your business you might have several such radars for different technologies (materials or medical tech, for example). The figure shows one of the four quadrants—techniques, platforms, tools, languages, and frameworks. The location on the rings of the radar indicate actions—adopt, trial, assess, hold.

- Adopt: Ready for use now. It has been proven through use on projects and general industry acceptance.
- Trial: Ready for cautious use. It is not completely proven, so use on carefully selected initiatives.
- Assess: Up and coming. It should be followed closely and used experimentally.
- Hold: Getting industry attention but not yet, or maybe ever, ready to use. It may be flawed, and might be viewed as something to avoid.

10. For the latest full radar, go to the ThoughtWorks website: www.thoughtworks.com.

Figure 2-3

An example of a ThoughtWorks tech radar (Vol. 19, 2018), techniques quadrant.

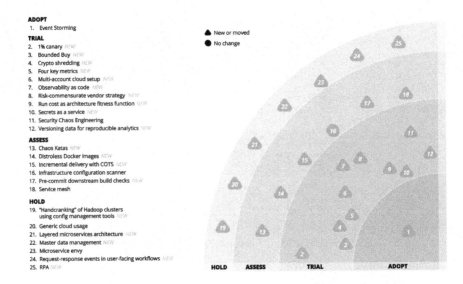

ADOPT
1. Event Storming

TRIAL
2. 1% canary *NEW*
3. Bounded Buy *NEW*
4. Crypto shredding *NEW*
5. Four key metrics *NEW*
6. Multi-account cloud setup *NEW*
7. Observability as code *NEW*
8. Risk-commensurate vendor strategy *NEW*
9. Run cost as architecture fitness function *NEW*
10. Secrets as a service *NEW*
11. Security Chaos Engineering
12. Versioning data for reproducible analytics *NEW*

ASSESS
13. Chaos Katas *NEW*
14. Distroless Docker images *NEW*
15. Incremental delivery with COTS *NEW*
16. Infrastructure configuration scanner
17. Pre-commit downstream build checks *NEW*
18. Service mesh

HOLD
19. "Handcranking" of Hadoop clusters using config management tools *NEW*
20. Generic cloud usage
21. Layered microservices architecture *NEW*
22. Master data management *NEW*
23. Microservice envy
24. Request-response events in user-facing workflows *NEW*
25. RPA *NEW*

▲ New or moved
● No change

HOLD   ASSESS   TRIAL   ADOPT

Probably the most important factor in building a tech radar and evaluating technologies is blending analysis with actual "use." While there are four actions on the radar, a couple of preliminary activities also exist: survey and investigate.

Survey is the process of identifying new technologies by gathering information from conferences, conversations, social media, analysis firms, professional papers, books (although books don't often come early enough), and Internet articles. This is the awareness stage—the point at which someone says, "Ah, we haven't heard about this before." This is the stage where you choose to go onto the next level or discontinue interest. After all, no one can afford to elevate every new technology to the next level of scrutiny.

At the investigate level, you continue gathering information from the sources mentioned previously and expand the search to include early adopters' experiences. In this activity, you are trying to answer questions about both business and technical viability. While the survey stage identifies something new, the investigate stage provides enough information to warrant potential addition to the radar.

"Could be a long week … Tech Radar creation, first session, blips unfiltered so far. Amazing how much changes in tech in 6 months!" (Tweet

from Mike Mason, Head of Technology for ThoughtWorks, during an early 2018 Radar update session)

In the assess stage (or action), you begin to try out the technology, mostly on internal experiments within the technology organization. At this point, you are assessing technical viability, rather than business viability. For example, you might play around with VR equipment to get a feel for the technology and its maturity. You might think about how it could be applied to your business, but wouldn't experiment with it yet.

During the trial stage, the technology could be used on carefully selected, and probably smaller, business initiatives. These trials should help determine whether the technology might move ahead to full adoption. You would continue to gather information from other users during this time to determine the pluses and minuses of the technology.

Once sufficient data is gathered from the trial stage and industry usage increases, you can then adopt the technology for wider use within your organization. Several factors, including how you can develop your capability (or buy it), influence the adopt decision.

At each of the levels, you ask critical questions relative to advancing the technology to the next level. Only a few will make it through each stage: Some will be abandoned, and some placed into a hold status. You need to limit work-in-progress (WIP) for each stage. Limit the number of things you're assessing or trialing at any one time, and make it clear to teams if another team is already assessing a technology so they can quickly ask and learn how that trial is going. This might be considered a kind of governance for learning.

Reducing Technical Debt

If your enterprise has been in existence for some time and has a large investment in legacy systems, how you manage technical debt will be a significant component of your technology strategy. Technical debt is the degradation of technology over time due to a lack of investment in maintaining adaptability and quality. It is similar to having a car that is not maintained, not even with oil changes, and therefore degrades over time—slows down, won't start, leaks oil. In software, developers may be forced to take shortcuts to make deadlines, testing isn't always rigorous, and periodic quick "fixes" can degrade code quality. Over the years, many legacy systems have delivered value to the business, but their technical debt accumulated to the point that even seemingly minor enhancements became difficult and time consuming. Figure 2-4 shows how this kind of degradation starts out slowly, but then accelerates as time passes.[11] More than a few legacy systems are now essentially unmaintainable. In the early days, changes are relatively easy. As technical debt grows, the answer to the question, "Do we implement new features or do we reduce technical debt?" is, of course skewed to new features. After a few years of ignoring technical debt, enhancements can take forever and you are faced with three equally bad options: rewrite the application (which is expensive and very risky), do nothing (and the problem gets worse and worse), or work toward reducing the technical debt systematically over time.

Limits to Growth

In the mid-2000s, Salesforce.com had a significant challenge: Its rapid growth was outpacing its software development delivery capability. The drag of its legacy system's technical debt and its software development process both contributed to the company's problems. But solving this multifaceted problem resulted in Salesforce being named by *Forbes* magazine as the most innovative company in the world for the years 2011–2015 (and in the top three since then). Salesforce credited its adoption of agile development practices as significantly contributing to the company's turnaround. Improving the quality of new code reduced the introduction of new tech debt, while introducing strategies for reducing legacy technical debt helped improve delivery times. Of course, this firm's success was the result of multiple business and technology factors, but introducing agility in its many forms was critical.

---

11. Highsmith, Jim. *Agile Project Management: Creating Innovative Products.* Boston: Addison-Wesley, 2010.

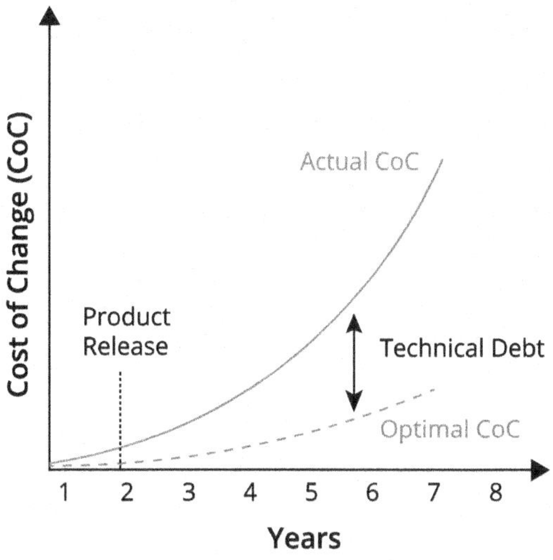

Figure 2-4
The impact of technical debt.

Cost of Change (CoC)

Actual CoC

Product
Release

Technical Debt

Optimal CoC

1 2 3 4 5 6 7 8

Years

A second problem with legacy systems is the difference in delivery cycle time between digital experience and legacy development groups. In less turbulent times, the fact that one of these groups was agile and operated on two-week delivery cycles and the other used traditional methods and operated on nine-month delivery cycles was a nuisance, but not debilitating. Today, that difference in delivery cycle time increasingly causes big problems. This disconnect is compounded by differences in release cycle times, particularly when continuous delivery is used in one case and not in the other.

Organizations are caught in a dilemma years in the making: Redeveloping the systems is too time consuming and risky, but building new digital assets depends on upgrades to these systems. Finding solutions to this dilemma—finding creative ways to revitalize these legacy systems by wrapping, selective revisions, and automated testing—becomes a critical piece of building new digital assets.[12]

12. For more on reducing technical debt, see Earle, George, and Mike Mason. "The Business Imperative to Modernize Your Tech Estate." *ThoughtWorks Insights*. https://www.thoughtworks.com/insights/blog/business-imperative-modernize-your-tech-estate.

Investment Decisions to Revitalize Core Enterprise Systems

You need to get creative about how to invest limited resources to revitalize core enterprise systems. An obvious choice, rewriting these systems, is an expensive and usually high-risk strategy—one to be pursued carefully. Fortunately, a wide range of options between doing nothing and rewriting are available—migrating to a services architecture (including microservices), evolutionary architecture, decoupling and wrapping, employing continuous delivery, and more.

It won't be enough to just get the delivery model right. Another reason why operational efficiency has taken priority over operational agility is the investment classification systems used in many enterprises. A number of classification schemes are used today, but they generally follow along the lines of that offered by MIT's Computer Information Systems Research group: infrastructure, transactional, informational, and strategic. In this scheme, perhaps 10 to 15 percent of the portfolio is deemed "strategic" and the rest is thought of as core enterprise systems, those where efficiency is king.

The need for agility in the Digital Age extends far beyond "strategic" systems, and revamping investment buckets is one way to emphasize this scope. What if we revise the scheme to reflect the new Digital Age reality, by including customer experience systems (a mobile app), customer experience support systems (order processing), internal support systems (accounting), and infrastructure (servers)? If we think of a scale that ranks needs from efficiency (1) to agility (5), then customer experience systems might need to be a 5, customer experience support systems a 3 or 4, internal support systems a 2, and infrastructure a 3.

Digital Technology Platforms

Platform is the latest buzzword. But is it more than just buzz? What exactly is a platform, and how does it amplify outcomes? Are there different types of platforms? In the simplest form, platforms are the assembly of components that achieve the leverage, or amplification, to keep up with the pace of change. Platforms come in two flavors: business and technology.

Business platforms are defined and described in *Platform Revolution: How Networking Markets Are Transforming the Economy and How to Make Them Work for You*, by Parker, Van Alstyne, and Choudary.[13] As an example, Airbnb utilizes a business platform to leverage the connection between customers and providers. Its platform offers customers far more rooms than traditional hotel chains, without the level of investment in bricks and mortar.

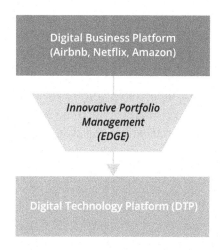

Figure 2-5
Platform and EDGE components.

Business platforms are enabled by digital technology platforms (DTP) as shown in Figure 2-5, you can have one without the other, though usually both are necessary in a digital enterprise. How are technology platforms different from traditional technology approaches such as enterprise architecture (EA)? IT organizations traditionally focused their EA on two related benefits—cost reductions and productivity improvements. DTP, however, has an entirely different fitness function—adaptability and delivery speed. DTP also has a much wider scope than traditional EA. Historically, cost pressure leads to standardization, which in turn leads to stagnation. In today's world, stagnation leads to—well, you know what it leads to. Within DTP, there is still a place for EA, but the "E" needs to change from "enterprise" to "evolutionary."[14]

13. Parker, Geoffrey G., Marshall W. Van Alstyne, and Sangeet Paul Choudary. *Platform Revolution: How Networking Markets Are Transforming the Economy and How to Make Them Work for You.* New York: W. W. Norton, 2016.
14. See for example, Ford, Neal, Rebecca Parsons, and Patrick Kua. *Building Evolutionary Architectures: Support Constant Change.* O'Reilly Media, 2017.

Focusing on cost drove organizations toward efficiency and productivity, which emphasize standardization as the chosen path to success. Your digital enterprise vision changes the emphasis to delivery speed and adaptability. For example, microservices help delivery teams customize their products, rather than standardize them. With the explosion of technology solutions, and more coming every day, standardization is a sure path to stagnation. Of course, there is a balance point between them: Unfettered customization can cause problems, but the goals of adaptability and speed drive platform design in different directions than cost-reduction efforts do.

A word about adaptability: In the pre-digital world, which focused on cost and productivity, the execution strategy became one of Plan–Do.[15] This strategy assumes that one knows, within somewhat narrow boundaries, what the future holds. If you understand the future, you can plan things like architectures and product features. All that's left is to execute the plan. Unfortunately, in our digital world (and often in our pre-digital world), we don't know the future—until it arrives. Our strategy needs to be one of Envision–Evolve. The vision, whether for an enterprise or a product, needs to be oriented toward customer value and outcomes. It provides direction, but allows for alternative paths to completion. Since the customers may "know it when they see it," the process needs to adjust time and time again to what we learn moving forward.

In our experience, the organizations that have been successful at digital transformation have unlocked their key assets by taking three steps:

- Removing friction from engineering teams
- Building an ecosystem around assets
- Experimenting efficiently and effectively with those assets

Removing Friction

Friction is usually considered as resistance to movement, but it can also be considered as a conflict between people. Whether it is described as resistance or conflict, friction slows us down. When you are blasting down a

15. The Plan–Do and Envision–Explore strategies are discussed further in Chapter 10, Adaptive Leadership.

ski slope on a mountain bike in the summer, friction can be a really good thing. However, friction within or external to a software delivery team isn't a good thing. Using self-sufficient teams reduces the friction between organizational units that would otherwise slow decision making. In software delivery, the friction between software development and operations organizations can slow the process to a crawl. The practices in DevOps have greatly reduced this source of friction. These practices are both organizational and technological—from using continuous integration technology to bridge the organizational gap between development and operations.

Friction can also arise from using the wrong technology for an initiative. Frequently new initiatives are forced to use inappropriate technology because of existing standards. For example, some early big data initiatives floundered because organizational standards required the use of traditional relational databases to manipulate unstructured data. Another example would be using a very heavyweight message queue implementation when something very simple would do nicely.

Agile practices encourage teams to deliver deployment-ready code every iteration and even deploy code if the team uses continuous deployment. One easy metric that provides an indication of how far away from that goal a team might be—essentially an indicator of how much friction is in the development process—is "the tail," referring to the time between freezing code development (it's never completely frozen) and product deployment. During this period, non-agile teams continue testing (especially integration), bug fixing, performance analysis, operations preparations, and more. Often we have encountered "tails" of 3 to 6 months or more in a 12-month deployment cycle. The longest tail we encountered was 18 months from "code complete" to deployment! As agile practices are implemented, you can watch this "tail" decrease as a measure of progress.

There are many ways to reduce friction that focus on removing barriers to faster delivery and improving adaptability. Another option is to correct the false tradeoff between speed and quality.

When you trade off more features for less quality, it's usually for a single release occurrence, not for an aggregation of releases over time. This practice is an outgrowth of waterfall development, in which intervals between releases were long, often a year or more, and trading new features for lower quality (say, poor design or less testing) obscured the cost and pushed consequences far into the future. When you have a large batch size (hundreds of features) and a long time frame (a year or more), the next releases (small maintenance or enhancements) are so trivial in relation to the first release that the feedback or impact of low quality is very difficult to determine.

In a waterfall project, it is easier to cut refactoring, for example, because the impact is felt in the future, when engineers feel the pain of technical debt and customers feel the pain of lengthy delivery schedules. Cycle time measures are irrelevant when release cycles are too long. However, as agile teams reduce delivery cycles to months, weeks, and days, the impact of poor quality becomes much easier to determine. When a team is running one-week deployment cycles, the effects of poor testing in one cycle may pop up quickly, in the next cycle or two. Poor design in one cycle begins to retard feature delivery in the next few cycles, so that the consequential feedback comes in a few weeks. If a team is measuring both feature throughput and cycle time, either or both can suffer quickly from software quality mediocrity.

Building an Asset Ecosystem

An ecosystem is a system or network of interconnecting and interacting parts. For example, the Apple iPhone thrived on an ecosystem of the hardware, operating system, and software developers and their "apps." We might also add the word "interdependent" to the definition of an ecosystem. Assets we think about in a platform strategy are data, hardware, software, capability, and thoughtware. Companies that grew up as digital companies—think about Google, Airbnb, and Netflix—have considered their platforms as ecosystems from the beginning. Similarly, they have built their digital platforms as strategic assets.

For long-time organizations with high technical debt, a strategy to rewrite existing software applications won't work—it's just too expensive. Plus, rewriting without making the necessary technical and organizational transformations is a waste of money. Your strategy needs to be a well-considered "layered" strategy where the layers are time. In 1995, Stewart Brand wrote an interesting book titled *How Buildings Learn: What Happens After They're Built*. Brand's premise was that the layers of a building change over time, at different rates. He envisions six building layers: site, structure, skin, services, space plan, and stuff. The structure, for example, changes at a very slow rate and is expensive to change; services (air conditioning and heating) change every 15 to 20 years and are moderately expensive; and stuff (furniture and fixtures) changes frequently and is inexpensive to change. Thinking of change in layers of time will assist you in tech strategy development.

As mentioned earlier, this analysis should be done in the spirit of agility—not an exhaustive analysis, but just enough to guide decision making. One of the tasks you need to complete is to determine a strategy for your key technology assets or asset classes. This analysis includes three components, shown in Figure 2-6: (1) determining the asset classes' impact on Lean Value Tree (LVT) goals, (2) speculating on the rate of change of this area of

Figure 2-6
Determining investment strategies for each asset or asset class.

the business, and (3) determining the current adaptability of asset classes.

First, look at each asset class and determine how integral this asset class is to implementing goals across the LVT:

- Impacts many goals (customer assets, for example)
- Impacts several goals
- Impacts very few goals

Second, for each business capability or product line, you need to anticipate the future rate of change:

- Extremely volatile
- Volatile

- Moderately volatile
- Relatively stable

Obviously, this analysis will be subject to change as the future unfolds, but making a relative assessment like this will help you develop an asset management strategy. Until you experiment with actual measurements such as cycle times, relative comparisons will be adequate. Especially for organizations with huge investments in legacy systems, prioritizing adaptability investments is critical.

The third stage of the asset analysis is to estimate the relative adaptability of each asset or asset class.

- Highly adaptable—relatively quick and inexpensive to change
- Adaptable—moderately expensive and time consuming to change
- Somewhat adaptable—difficult and expensive to change
- Not adaptable—very expensive and time consuming to change

Having these three estimates of the need to adapt, the rate of change, and the ability to adapt helps to determine strategy. For example, an asset that is critical to implementing a number of goals in an extremely volatile business environment and whose adaptability is very expensive and time consuming to change is obviously on the "critical" list. An asset whose business environment is relatively stable, that is used in only one goal, and whose adaptability is expensive and time consuming would have a very low priority.

This kind of asset analysis is particularly important when you are prioritizing legacy systems that support Business as Usual (BAU) and trying to reduce technical debt.

Experimenting

One of the premises of EDGE is that adaptation requires experimentation, and for that experimentation to succeed, you need an experimental mindset, an experimental process, and experimental tools. Rather than planning, which indicates a prescriptive solution, you need to think of the future in terms of hypotheses about the future. You then test those hypotheses with short-cycle experiments.

The cultural mindset is one of exploration—that you can't know everything in advance and that significant deviations are the norm. The cultural aspects of experimentation are covered in more depth in Chapter 10. The second requirement is an experimental process, which for the purposes of this book is an enhanced version of agile. The third requirement is that you need a platform, the right technology components, to experiment rapidly. These components need to cover the entire development life cycle, from spinning up development environments rapidly to effective continuous integration tools.

You need these technology components for every type of development—legacy back-office systems, online applications, mobile applications, big data and analytical systems, and applications with an Internet of Things (IoT) piece.

Who Creates Your Technology Strategy?

Who works on your technology strategy is more important than the strategy itself. Years ago, Jim was working with a CMM level 5[16] organization in India. Like any organization at that CMM level, it had extensive processes, each with abundant documentation. However, the firm relayed a recent problem. For a project using a technology (Microsoft's .NET) that was new to the team, the staff conducted a technical review, getting team members and others involved. They dutifully followed the process steps and completed all the required documentation, but subsequently the project ran into severe technical difficulties. It turned out that while they had a "good" process, no one on the review team had any experience with .NET. In other words, they had the process, but not the expertise. As the Agile Manifesto says, "individuals and interactions over process and tools."[17] Having the right people involved in your technology strategy is imperative.

---

16. CMM refers to the Capability Maturity Model developed by the Software Engineering Institute. The CMM is a highly process-oriented model.
17. "Manifesto for Agile Software Development." The Agile Manifesto, 2001. http://agilemanifesto.org/.

Make no mistake: Building a tech radar (and, in fact, the entire tech strategy) is not inexpensive. At ThoughtWorks, we bring together more than 20 tech experts, from all over the world, at least twice a year for a week to argue, debate, and decide on what goes on the radar, what comes off, and where items are placed. Certain collaborations need to take place face-to-face, and this is one of them. ThoughtWorks staff have hundreds of cutting-edge projects from which to draw data, providing a depth of working knowledge about these radar items.

Here is one fairly simple way of selecting people to work on your tech radar and other technology strategy components: Look at your development teams and ask the question, "Who is so critical to this team (or teams) that we can't possibly do without them for a week?" That's who you should pick. If you can't break key people loose to work on the radar and other components, then don't bother. You will end up like the .NET technical review team in the story—having a process without content. Gazing into the future is tricky, even for the best of us.

At ThoughtWorks, we encourage the concept of "thought leaders"—leaders in the industry who are respected by their peers.[18] You can use a similar concept of "thought leaders" within your enterprise—individuals who are respected by peers within your enterprise and possibly externally.

So merit, expertise, and respect top the list of traits wanted on your tech evaluation team. You want people who have product delivery experience, not just staff experience. You want diversity—junior and senior, male and female, different hierarchy levels, and geographic locations. You need to know what's cooking in Silicon Valley, but also in Bangalore, Beijing, Munich, and Manchester—especially if your company is international.

One point we need to make about tech strategy, radar, and shifts is that you can't buy them. At least, you can't buy all of them. For example, you might buy an analyst firm's tech evaluation as part of your investigation process, but you need to have the technical expertise to evaluate and determine how to use that technology.

In the 1990s and into the twenty-first century, when outsourcing of major IT components was popular, some companies discovered they had

---

18. Within ThoughtWorks, a company of 5000-plus people in 2018, there are authors of more than 80 books.

outsourced far too much of the expertise they needed just to manage the agreements. This was the era when IT was considered a cost center, not a value center. "We can outsource payroll, so why not IT?," the thinking went. But you can't outsource your transformation to a digital enterprise—you have to be more involved.

However, you can partner, which is very different from outsourcing. Look ahead to Figure 9-1, which shows the three dimensions of interaction—compliance, cooperation, and collaboration. Outsourcing was often a compliance relationship in which each party spelled out their relationship in excruciatingly detailed contracts. Even these detailed contracts failed, in many instances, to deliver the service that companies expected. A compliance relationship is one of low trust, which leaves little room for innovation and creativity—whether with internal or external parties.

Delivering innovative, customer-value–oriented products demands a high-trust, collaborative relationship between business and IT. Iterative, experimental processes focused on value delivery require a different mindset about "plans" and "contracts." Teams need to adjust and adapt over time as experiments provide new learning. Trying to write a detailed, specific, compliance-based contract would be a waste of time in this environment.

Final Thoughts

Embracing Tech@Core should be a centerpiece of your digital transformation. That technology is a critical piece of becoming a digital enterprise isn't a new revelation. What is different, however, is the degree to which technology needs to permeate every aspect of planning for your future. Fifty to sixty years ago, when IT was in its infancy, the understanding of how technology might impact organizations was vested in the minds of the technology specialists of the time, and they struggled with how these newfangled computer capabilities might be used.

Over the years, the gap in technology knowledge between technology and business groups gradually shrank. Today, it has become imperative to integrate this knowledge into the fabric of organizational life.

Chapter 3

EDGE Principles

A digital transformation demands two key ingredients—articulated principles and trust in leaders.

From the beginning, the agile and lean movements have been more about principles than practices, processes, or tools. It's not that these latter three are unimportant. Rather, by focusing on the principles, you're better able to make agile and lean work for you. By focusing on principles, you can better build a responsive enterprise. In his book *Good to Great: Why Some Companies Make the Leap and Others Don't*, Jim Collins points out the need to preserve and the need to change. You need to preserve core values and purpose, and that foundation creates the stability required to change culture, practices, and goals. Without core values or principles, there isn't an anchor from which to make critical decisions about change.

The Agile Manifesto has been the inspiration for agile development for nearly 20 years. It lays out the agile principles, and you can then successfully adapt the right practices or tools for your organization. A common misconception about building enterprise responsiveness is that there is a recipe—a clear set of steps that can be followed, so that at the end the organization is "agile." There isn't one recipe to follow. Each organization is different, as is its environment. The principles of EDGE enable all the parts of the organization to adopt practices and tools, not just software delivery teams.

Trust in leaders is essential because in the midst of change, when everyone in your organization is nervous and uncertain about the future—their future, people need to feel safe. Some pundits in the agile community openly advise that in an agile transition as many as one-third of your staff and management won't make the grade. How "safe" do you suppose staff will feel if they think one-third of them will be terminated or relegated to the worst jobs? How excited will anyone be about the transition? Trust in management means that people feel their jobs will stay intact even though their roles will change. It means that leaders and managers engage the staff so they are more comfortable in their discomfort. People who don't feel safe, for whatever reason, will be resistant to change. Chapter 10, Adaptive Leadership, addresses adaptive leadership behaviors that lead to a safer tech environment. Of course, a few people won't make the grade—that is inevitable. But this realization is far different than starting the transformation process by stating a large number of people won't be retained. When thinking about the technology talent and capabilities needed for your transformation, try a capability building mindset rather than emphasizing termination.

Safety Is a Key Cultural Trait

"Within the last year, I've found a new passion, direction, and metaphor.

I call it *tech safety*.

Tech safety leads us to reduce or remove injuries in our high-tech lives.

Such injuries aren't cuts, burns, or fatalities.

High-tech injuries are cognitive, emotional, financial, and secondarily physical.

Whether you make, use, or consume high-tech products and services, tech safety improves your life by discovering hazards and removing or reducing your injuries."

—Joshua Kerievsky,[1] *Industrial Logic, Tech Safety Blog,* posted June 13, 2013

Your ability to adapt EDGE practices, based on an understanding of the principles, will be critical to success. The six guiding principles outlined in this chapter (Figure 3-1) are key to understanding and applying EDGE. These principles help us answer questions about investing for change, working together, and adapting quickly.

1. Josh has been a leader in the agile movement and in fostering the ideas around tech safety.

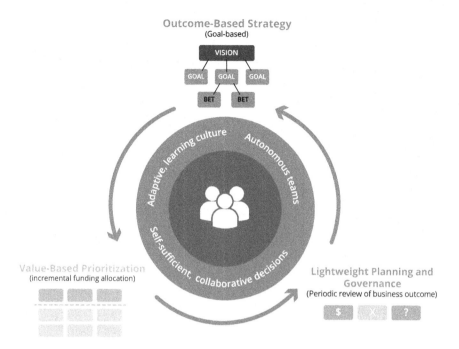

Figure 3-1
Principles of EDGE.

The three principles on the outside loop—outcome-based strategy, value-based prioritization, and lightweight planning and governance— focus on answering the "how should we invest" question. The inner loop principles—autonomous teams; adaptive, learning culture; and self-sufficient, collaborative decisions—speak to working together and adapting fast enough. But in reality, the relationships between the key questions and principles are multifaceted. Lightweight governance, for example, also helps define how teams work together.

When scaling agile and lean methods, there's often a disconnect as the scaled versions attempt to create a prescriptive structure or process rather than an adaptive one. We believe that your decision-making framework is more important than detailed processes.

Outcome-Based Strategy

Enterprises undertake transformations to respond to changes in their environment. One of the more difficult things for managers and executives to embrace in these transformations is learning to measure success differently.

As your organization learns from its environment, you'll want to invest more in the ideas that yield the most promise in furthering your vision. Traditionally, teams have been rewarded for performing against metrics that don't necessarily relate to business outcomes. For example, many organizations gauge their progress toward a goal by whether a design or schedule gate has been met. While these things may (or may not) help guide teams, they are not themselves valuable to a customer.

"This outcome orientation will drive you to a different way of thinking and different ways of delivering value."
—John Buhl, Principal, Lean Enterprise Transformation, Vanguard (Money 20/20 Conference, 2016)

EDGE advocates investing based on customer outcomes (customer value) first, and business benefits (i.e., profit, market share) second. Once these value-based outcomes and their measures of success and targets have been established and shared, it's far more effective to align groups to them. You can then use performance against these targets to decide to invest more, stop investing altogether, or pivot to a new, perhaps related, opportunity.

Value-Based Prioritization

Prioritization decisions should be based on value, and value should be defined in a way that makes sense for your enterprise. EDGE uses the term "value" to represent customer value: what a customer is willing to pay for. Healthcare organization customers may value patient outcomes and safety; public services customers may value responsiveness; commercial entity customers may value customer satisfaction. However your organization defines customer value, it's important to measure based on that value and to make investment decisions accordingly.

Measures of Success (MoS, covered in Chapter 5, Measuring and Prioritizing Value) should represent value at every level, from organizational goals to detailed implementation stories, so people don't end up working at cross purposes. Those measurements are important for demonstrating incremental progress of value creation and to drive prioritization to ensure you are working on the most valuable things first. Work can be quickly reprioritized based on value as new information becomes available. This value-based approach to prioritization maintains alignment throughout the organization. If a new idea is created as you learn about the customer's needs, you can quickly compare it to the existing work in progress and adjust priorities.

Lightweight Planning and Governance

The Digital Age requires a better business–technology partnership to translate ideas into value and to reduce the wasted efforts that often accompany excessive process and documentation. In EDGE, governance is built on agile and lean principles, from vision to delivery. Governance provides a framework to ensure that:

- Customer value goals are being met within established constraints (time, cost, and internal and external regulatory requirements).
- Decision-making rights required for accountability are effectively allocated and managed.

Decision-making rights are particularly important in EDGE because autonomous teams take on greater decision making and accountability. The governance bodies must carefully balance the goal of giving autonomous teams greater decision authority while maintaining their fiduciary responsibilities. This could also be considered a balance of guidance and oversight.

Many governance systems, notably traditional phase-gate ones, focus on exhaustive documentation artifacts and heavyweight processes that introduce intolerable delays. Their emphasis is on process, rather than on speedy decision making. Governance teams need to navigate a paradox—ensuring adequate compliance to fiduciary, regulatory, and risk management needs while also moderating the burdensome overhead of traditional governance processes.

When teams are asked to be flexible, adaptive, and agile, governance processes need to mirror those goals. This means changing the measurement systems to be more outcome oriented. It doesn't require abandoning traditional cost and schedule measures, but it does mean subordinating them to measures of customer value.

Adaptive, Learning Culture

Can your organization adapt fast enough? This is a fundamental question today, for every organization, every enterprise. But it's not enough to have agile delivery teams or continuous delivery: To be "fast enough," your enterprise must have a responsive technology platform, an experimental and learning culture, and an executive team dedicated to finding the right balance between adapting and planning (most executives are still far too enamored with planning).

One of the misconceptions of traditional planning is the idea that risk can be reduced if an enterprise thinks thoroughly about a target end state and plans risk-mitigation steps for every conceivable event along the way. In the old, slower world, these "Plan–Do" approaches, in which everything was planned up front, worked, sort of. But today, you need an "Envision–Explore" approach that encourages innovation and exploration, adjusting and pivoting, as reality overtakes plans. Traditional approaches tried to "plan" away uncertainty. *EDGE's approach is to experiment away uncertainty.*

EDGE advocates building quick, incremental feedback from the real world into the process. The feedback loops should have a cadence of weeks or months—after all, your enterprise can't wait years to determine whether plans deliver. These explorations are also a great way to reduce risk. Short-duration, low-cost experiments provide valuable feedback, where learning is embraced as an outcome. As much can be learned from an idea that fails as can be learned from one that succeeds. For example, for start-up companies, finding the right product–market fit may take a couple of years of experimenting. Thinking that you can determine product–market fit internally and then build such a product usually sets your organization on a long, expensive path to failure.

Adaptive leaders need to create an environment in which people feel confident enough to engage in experimentation and adjustment. They need to lead the change process to relieve anxiety and motivate people to try new solutions, to be bold in their vision of what can be accomplished, to be persistent in achieving that vision, and to inspire others to make the journey with them.

Autonomous Teams

In fast-paced, short-iteration delivery cycles, teams don't have time to confirm every decision with a management hierarchy or with functional specialists. In this environment, teams should have broad decision-making authority and be accountable for outcomes delivered—not just delivery of features. Autonomous teams are creative, collaborative, innovative, and empowered—and sometimes messy and unruly.

Enabling Autonomy

We were working with a global insurance organization whose leadership team was experiencing poor results from its traditional approach to change. The organization's approach involved leadership and management locking themselves in a room every quarter and devising plans on exactly what they wanted to change, so that each leader walked out of the session with a clear directive to teams.

"When we told teams what to do, we got limited results."

The chief digital officer of the Netherlands division tried a different approach. He chose a small, cross-functional team and gave them a goal: help our organization deliver value, more quickly. This team collaborated over five days. On the third day, they called the chief digital officer with a very important question:

"In our proposed approach, there are no managers. Is that a problem?"

"No," he said. "Help me understand how, under this new approach, you will meet your goals, and how we measure the impact, and I will support you."

They proposed to reduce the scope of the team's responsibility. They found teams had problems with a large scope and were unable to clear a pathway to move forward because the problem was just too big.

"During our analysis, we found that teams that had very large boundaries and too much ambiguity took a long time to converge on a solution. Teams that had more focused accountabilities and clear guardrails where they could operate could get to the delivery of value a lot faster."

So what is the key to autonomy? We think it's the delicate balance between self-directing work and accountability. This balance occurs when teams understand the desired outcome and their decision rights and have the resources necessary to be successful. Traditional functional teams had so many stakeholders—which meant waiting for some manager or functional group to make a decision—that they felt no sense of accountability. Conversely, some agile teams have run wild, making decisions they shouldn't. Striking the right balance between decision making and accountability isn't easy, but necessary for creating effective autonomous teams.

Characteristics of Autonomous Teams

The best decisions and products result from teams with the following characteristics:

- **Independent.** Teams are self-directed with clear goals and boundaries they can play within.
- **Empowered.** Teams perceive that their decisions aren't constantly questioned; they have a clear understanding of their decision rights.
- **Accountable.** Teams feel responsible for the outcomes they've agreed to.
- **Collaborative.** There is a high degree of trust within the team, and team members feel comfortable speaking their minds and working together.
- **Interdisciplinary.** Different disciplines contribute to better solutions and better decisions by bringing diverse perspectives and experiences.
- **Transparent.** Information is widely distributed and shared, not withheld.

Self-Sufficient, Collaborative Decision Making

Traditional hierarchical management's desire for control can impede decision making and result in poor choices. The best and quickest decisions are made by those closest to the work. EDGE provides a means for responsibly delegating decisions to people who are closest to the information.[2]

EDGE also helps organizations set up feedback mechanisms to ensure that even though many decisions are made at the team level, decisions are transparent; this enables leaders to guide teams. Part of the reason for insisting on short iterations and frequent cadence of feedback is to ensure that teams aren't going too long without showing their thinking and what they've accomplished. An organization can be far more responsive by setting up guard rails for making good decisions and allowing a group to operate freely within those boundaries.

Transparency means that funding decisions and the rationale for those decisions are freely shared at all levels of the organization—from executives to delivery teams. Goal decisions, for example, form a context for making decisions about bets and initiatives. When the teams know why those goals were chosen, and even which ones were discussed and not selected, they make better decisions about how to achieve those goals.

Collaborative decision making doesn't mean everyone is involved in each and every decision, but rather that the process includes those whom the decision impacts. Furthermore, better decisions, at all levels, arise from a common understanding of the desired business outcomes.

Final Thoughts

Processes, practices, tools, and even people change over time. Principles, by contrast, evolve slowly, if at all. Principles become the bedrock from which change can spring. As subsequent chapters delve into processes and practices, they will add more depth to the EDGE principles.

2. See Chapter 9, Autonomous Teams and Collaborative, for the difference between cross-functional and self-sufficient teams.

Chapter 4

Building a Value-Driven Portfolio

One of the fundamental questions raised by EDGE is "How should we invest?" In Chapters 1, The Big Picture, and 2, Tech@Core, we discussed the vast opportunities for organizations today, brought about in large measure by advances in technology. Every enterprise, from the smallest to the largest, must sift through these opportunities to come up with focused goals—which opportunities to pursue, which opportunities to consider further in the future, and which opportunities to abandon. As you know from experience, this is not an easy process. It requires skillful analytical ability and keen judgment. The Lean Value Tree (LVT) and Measures of Success (MoS) introduced in this and the next chapter offer thought-enhancing tools to assist in this process. But the phrase "keen judgment" shouldn't be taken lightly: This and the next chapter outline a process for investing in your digital enterprise, but all the LVT charts in the world won't make up for poor judgment. There is no magic formula for transforming your organization. Perhaps we need to add a caveat to our quest for courageous executives: They need good judgment as well as courage.

The investment question has three stages. First, determine what to invest in. We start this process by articulating the business vision and strategy as an LVT of goals, bets, and initiatives. Second, develop actionable, outcome-oriented MoS that clearly indicate progress *as the delivery process unfolds*, not at the end. Third, use the relative value of those MoS to prioritize work on the LVT items. Stage 1 is addressed in this chapter, and stages 2 and 3 are covered in Chapter 5, Measuring and Prioritizing Value.

The word "tree" in the concept "Lean Value Tree" is important. Trees have branches that evolve from the trunk (vision). Trees are living things that change and adapt to environmental conditions. Your LVT isn't a planning document that sits on the shelf behind your desk gathering dust. Instead, it is leadership's vision of the future—from its trunk to its leaves—that everyone in your organization can point to and say, "We are going that way, and I understand why."

As a living document, the LVT provides a line-of-sight to the strategic intent of the organization and, therefore, becomes critical input to decision making through the entire value stream. When done well, this tool closes the traditional gap between strategic plans that are well understood by the executives and the decision making of the people in each value stream that actually steers the business on a day-to-day basis.

Once work is under way, you apply value-driven, short-iteration, lightweight governance to steer the portfolio of investments toward the stated vision. The LVT becomes the linkage of the organization's steering mechanism that grounds decisions in an understanding of the strategic intent and desired outcomes.

A Telco Lean Value Tree

During our first iteration of the Lean Value Tree with the digital business of a telecommunications company, we did an initial two-hour timeboxed assessment with the director of digital products and portfolio owner, initially to evaluate our knowledge of the current portfolio.

We started by mapping all current work in progress against the goals of the business. During this exercise, we discovered the goals didn't articulate why they were important for the organization. For example, "Drive to 20% market share" didn't express how customers would benefit from this investment. So we spent some time understanding how each of the items in the portfolio aligned to the organizational goals. From this exercise, we were able to reframe the work in flight into groups of customer outcome initiatives. For instance, "Drive to 20% market share" became "Enable customers to seamlessly view live TV and Internet TV all in one place."

We learned three things from this timeboxed exercise:

1. By articulating the organizational goals in terms of customer outcomes, it became really clear what the value of each investment was and why it was important for the organization.

2. By visualizing all work in flight, we could see that the least important initiatives were receiving the most amount of funding. This led to opportunities to rebalance the portfolio to deliver the greatest value for customers.

3. By timeboxing the initial portfolio review, we were able to demonstrate the value of applying EDGE and build the case for continuing this work with the portfolio owners, business unit leads, and chief digital officer.

Strategy and the Lean Value Tree

The LVT tool is used to capture and share your organizational vision and strategy. Everything in the tree stems from the executive business vision and is framed in terms of outcomes, so the value those activities will provide to the organization is clear. In Chapter 1, we introduced the concept of fitness functions and making the transition from focusing on return on investment (ROI) and related measures to first focusing on the outcome measured by customer value. As you proceed to build your LVT, keep this mantra in mind: "Outcomes, customer, value."

The LVT, as shown in Figure 4-1, embraces the value-driven practices of lean development, as all work stems from the vision and clearly links to goals. There are no special side projects or huge programs of work. Instead, work is broken down into small, independently valuable increments that clearly tie back to an outcome. The value of each incremental outcome should be measurable.

Figure 4-1
The Lean Value Tree
enables you to capture
and share your vision
and strategy.

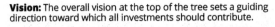

Vision: The overall vision at the top of the tree sets a guiding direction toward which all investments should contribute.

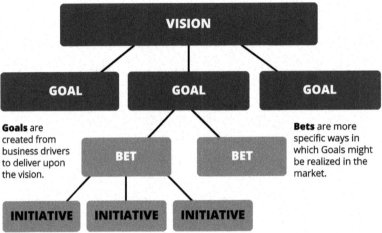

Goals are created from business drivers to deliver upon the vision.

Bets are more specific ways in which Goals might be realized in the market.

Initiatives are actions to deliver tangible value. Initiatives have a clear customer need and business opportunity defined.

Example: Lean Value Tree is a visual tool to facilitate capturing and sharing an organizational vision and strategy.

A Note about Terminology

The label descriptions used here to illustrate the LVT are just one example of how it's described in practice. Some alternative labels work equally well, however. You should adjust your use of the terminology of the LVT to your environment. Bets might be a good way to describe a hypothesis of value in the entertainment industry, but might not be appropriate in a financial advice setting.

The number of levels in the tree is also flexible for the environment. Three levels is typical to describe an organization-wide portfolio, but you could potentially have only two levels, or as many as four.

Here are some examples of LVT labels we have applied in practice:

- Goals, bets, initiatives
- Outcomes, initiatives, minimum viable product (MVP)
- Objectives, themes, hypothesis
- Goals, hypothesis, promises of value
- Big rocks, boulders, pebbles
- L1, L2, L3 (levels)

Defining Goals, Bets, and Initiatives

Goals

The structure of goals, bets, and initiatives is shown in Figure 4-2. A goal describes how the organization intends to realize the vision. Goals are relatively stable views of the high-level business strategy and are expressed in terms of desired outcomes, rather than specific solutions, product ideas, or features. Ideally, goals articulate the desired customer outcome that will enable the organization to achieve its vision. Goals should provide some visibility into the organization's course for the next one to three years. This doesn't mean goals will not change during that period, but they should be ambitious enough to encourage longer-term thinking and the stability that brings to the organization's decision making.

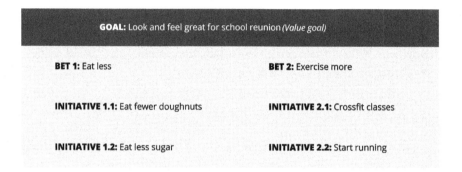

Figure 4-2
An example LVT for improving health and weight loss.

Bets

A goal consists of a portfolio of bets. Each bet is a hypothesis of value that the organization believes will help it realize a goal. If bets don't support achieving the goal, they don't belong in the portfolio. Conversely, every bet necessary to achieve the goal belongs together under the goal in the tree. In this way, we establish the mutually exclusive, collectively exhaustive (MECE)[1] nature of the LVT. An enterprise can continue to invest in the bets that further a goal and cease to invest in those that don't.

1. Minto, Barbara. *The Pyramid Principle: Logic in Writing and Thinking.* 3rd ed. Harlow, UK: Prentice Hall, 2010.

So, why do we like the term "bet"? In *Adaptive Software Development,*[2] Jim Highsmith introduced a similar term, "speculate." We use these terms in place of the term "plan" to indicate that the future is unknown and often even unknowable until you get there. A "plan" has been viewed by many in the past as deterministic: If we plan it well enough, we should expect reality to work out the way we planned it. "Bet" and "speculate" force us to face the reality that the future will bring changes that we didn't anticipate. If we admit that the future will be variable, then we have to put better practices and measures of success in place that enable us to adapt to the future that occurs.

> *In a complex environment, following a plan produces the product you intended, just not the product that you need.*
>
> —Jim Highsmith

We believe that accepting this fundamental truth—that the future is unknowable and that your systems for decision making must be adaptive—is essential for success in today's complex environment. Organizations with courageous leaders that face an uncertain future and forge ahead anyway will ultimately outperform their competitors.

Initiatives

An initiative describes what to build to prove out a bet. Initiatives typically take the form of a series of smaller hypotheses (or experiments) that have a clear measure of success, based on which teams can make decisions on whether they're able to prove or disprove the hypothesis.

An initiative differs from a project, in that projects typically spin up and ramp down to execute a plan and build features within a fixed end-date, whereas initiatives have a running backlog of hypotheses that are continuously reprioritized. Completion is defined by achieving the desired outcomes, rather than by completing all the activities in the plan. This is a very important mindset change—from focusing on outputs to focusing on outcomes.[3]

---

2. Highsmith, James A. *Adaptive Software Development: A Collaborative Approach to Managing Complex Systems.* New York: Dorset House, 1999.

3. Chapter 6, Building a Product Mindset, covers this topic in more detail.

Describing a Value-Driven Portfolio

Each node (goal, bet, or initiative) of the LVT describes a portfolio; the linkages between each node show which nodes are related to each other. Each is also described by MoS that represent the desired outcome and some additional descriptive information that helps everyone in the organization understand the intent behind it. The following guidelines suggest which information should be represented at the goal, bet, and initiative level. This information should be visual, should be easily accessible to anyone in the organization, and lays the foundation for successful governance during periodic value reviews.

A portfolio node (a goal example is shown in Figure 4-3) for a goal, bet, or initiative should:

- Have a name
- Identify its relationship to other nodes
- Have a goal owner or owner team
- Have a description (expressed as a desired outcome)
- Identify potential challenges and opportunities
- Have one to three measures of success
- Identify potential subnodes

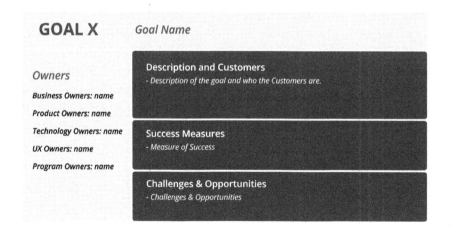

Figure 4-3

Example 1 page description of a strategic goal.

Strategic Portfolio Ownership

Now, with clearly defined portfolios, you can delegate decision rights for each portfolio (i.e., each node in the LVT) to those people who are best equipped to make the decisions required to achieve the desired outcome. EDGE recommends moving decisions as close to the work as possible, so we offer the following guidelines for ownership and decision rights of the various portfolio levels.

The executive team should create the vision and goal levels of the LVT. This aligns well with their typical responsibilities of developing strategy and allocating investment to support that strategy. As mentioned earlier, vision and goals should be relatively stable and provide the foundation for communicating the strategic intent of the organization. In our steering mechanism metaphor, this is the rudder that allows the executive team to steer the organization.

For each goal in the strategic portfolio described by the executive team, a goal team is created. This team should have representation from at least the business operations, technology, and product organizations. The charter of this team is to define the portfolio of bets that constitute the goal for which they have been granted accountability. This is often not a full-time job for the individual team members, and the likely candidates for these roles will vary depending upon the organization. The intent is to have representation from the whole value stream involved in the strategic decisions to invest in and prioritize the portfolio. This is critical to lay the foundation for accountability. The goal team owns responsibility for the outcome, rather than for the execution of a plan. If their first ideas about the bets that will achieve the desired outcome of the goal are not working, it is their responsibility to change the bets and invest in something that will, albeit within the bounds of the investment that was granted to them for the goal from the executive team.

For each bet in the goal portfolio described by the goal team, a bet team is created. Again, representation from the entire value stream is important, and the accountability and decision rights are similar to those of the goal team, which is situated one level up in the tree. You then create a portfolio of initiatives and determine the MoS and investment allocation for them.

For each initiative in the bet portfolio described by the bet team, responsibility is delegated to an initiative team. Here, we finally connect to people who will actually execute the work. As initiatives are funded by the bet team, they are assigned to a delivery team to execute.[4] For now, we will focus on the owner-ship of the initiative and the sources of the constraints. The delivery team makes the decisions within the initiative and is accountable to the bet team to produce the desired outcome (MoS) within the bounds of the funding granted by them.

This cascading delegation, shown in Figure 4-4, with alignment to the level above, borrows heavily from the lean movement's Hoshin Kanri.[5] In particular, the concept of "catchball" emphasizes communication, account-ability, and feedback between layers of responsibility in the organization. This approach differs to some extent from the original top-down nature of Hoshin Kanri and encourages a more collaborative development of various portfolio elements as a way to tap into the hive mind of an organization as well as to drive buy-in from a change management perspective.[6]

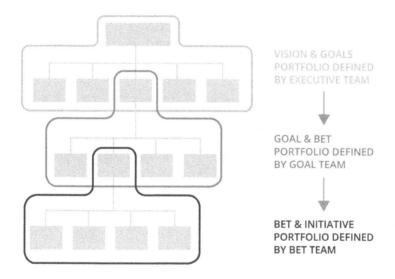

VISION & GOALS
PORTFOLIO DEFINED
BY EXECUTIVE TEAM

GOAL & BET
PORTFOLIO DEFINED
BY GOAL TEAM

BET & INITIATIVE
PORTFOLIO DEFINED
BY BET TEAM

Figure 4-4
Cascading ownership of portfolios.

All work within an organization's strategic portfolio is aligned to further its vision through the LVT. An organization uses the LVT to share key informa-tion (investment allocations, measures of success and alignment) in one place so that it is easily available and understood. Responsibility and accountability

---

4. Described further in Chapter 9, Autonomous Teams and Collaborative Decision Making.
5. Akao, Yoji. *Hoshin Kanri: Policy Deployment for Successful TQM*. New York: Productivity Press, 2017.
6. The accountability side of this system is discussed in Chapter 8, Lightweight Governance.

are clear to everyone in the organization, and decision rights are as close to the work as possible to ensure maximum context and minimum delays.

Eating Our Own Dog Food

At ThoughtWorks, we experiment with new ways of working within our own organization to learn and evolve what we offer to clients. During our early application of EDGE for our technology operations team, we decided the LVT should represent only the strategic initiatives that were considered new to the organization. This enabled us to focus on achieving the desired ROI from the limited investment dollars we were able to allocate to innovative new offerings.

In other words, we left Business as Usual (BAU) activities out. This has a knock-on effect. Teams that were working on BAU felt their work wasn't valued, because it wasn't visible. Despite management efforts to assure teams that their work really was valued, the perception did not change. EDGE states: "A business cannot value what it cannot see," so we decided to make the entire portfolio visible (incorporating BAU[7]). This supported deeper tradeoffs, enabling us to free up people to work on more valuable things.

—*Mark Pearson, Value Management Office,*
TechOps ThoughtWorks

Evolving the Lean Value Tree

The executive team is responsible for adding new goals or revising goals on the LVT. Trees grow new limbs from time to time, sometimes in places you didn't expect. Goals, like limbs, should be regularly reviewed, and should be modified or removed when market insights change or are added as new opportunities emerge. The value realization team (VRT)[8] and the executive team collaborate on these changes, using the periodic value review as the primary forum for these discussions.

7. See more about incorporating BAU in Chapter 7, Integrating Strategic and Business as Usual Portfolios.
8. The VRT evolved from a portfolio management office and is explained further in Chapter 9.

Adding a New Goal

New goals can arise from multiple channels:

- Strategic planning: industry, competitor, and customer analysis
- Feedback from bet owners and their teams
- Executive vision and inspiration

Potential goals should be examined in depth by a preliminary goal owner team and staffed with people who can bring different experiences and domain perspectives. That goal owner team should develop a broad view of the goal and make initial observations on possible bets and MoS. By doing so, it can develop and share high-level insights. This information enables the executive team to decide whether to take on this goal.

Once a potential goal is well understood, the organization has multiple options available:

- Add it as a new goal to the LVT
- Merge it with an existing goal
- Add it as a strategic bet under an existing goal
- Send it back to the preliminary owner team for further development
- Drop the goal
- Keep it on the goal or bet backlog for future consideration

Goals adopted by the organization need a permanent ownership team that's responsible for adjusting the bets and MoS as needed and for reviewing the strategy developed by the preliminary team.

Adding a New Bet or Initiative

EDGE is fractal. Consequently, the process for adding a new bet is very similar to that for adding a new goal: identification, intake by the VRT, review by a preliminary owner team, promotion to a backlog candidate, and then placement onto the LVT (Figure 4-5).

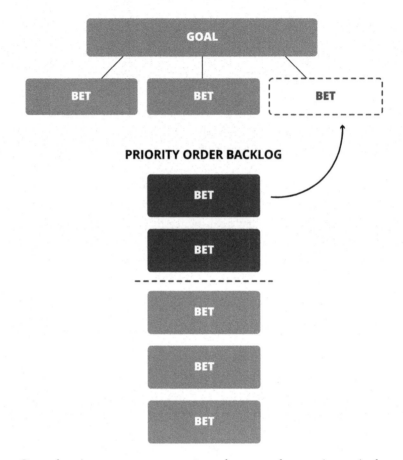

Figure 4-5
New bets must be relatively ranked against other bets in the backlog. The highest value bet gets moved onto the tree first.

Once there's agreement on moving a bet onto the tree (or not), the goal owners can decide when to create the bet owner team and do more detailed work.

Bets should be reviewed and updated more frequently than goals. They can be added, eliminated, or adjusted based on progress (or lack thereof), changes in relative value ranking with other bets on the backlog, or expansion of the scope or funding for a goal.

The proposal process is repeated again for initiatives within bets—just as it was for bets within goals. The exception for initiatives is that new work could also be sustaining items.

The updated LVT and supporting details should be common working knowledge at all levels of an organization. The publishing of that information is coordinated by the VRT and requires executive team and owner participation to evangelize and explain how things have changed and why.

Funding Allocation

Determining the best opportunity to pursue can be a daunting choice. There's always a temptation to favor immediate and urgent needs over future opportunities, or one business area over another. After all, investment in current products and services seems less risky; ROI more attainable. But for long-term success, your executive team needs to allocate its investment for specific goals, within set timescales, adjusting on the basis of measured results.

In EDGE, the executive team determines target levels of investment (see Figure 4-6) for each goal as a proportion of their overall strategic investment. This ensures that the total investment is balanced across the overall goals. Further allocation to the bet and initiative levels is shown in Figure 4-7. With smaller organizations, investment breakdown by goals may be sufficient. Larger or more complex organizations may need to allocate investments by goals and categories. For example, an international organization may need to allocate investments to geography (a "category") and then goals. Once funds are allocated to categories, then you can proceed to prioritize a list of goals.

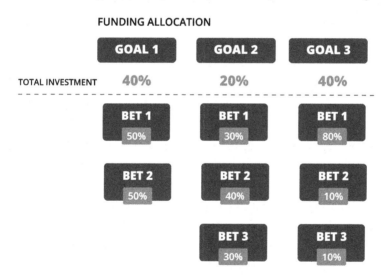

FUNDING ALLOCATION

Figure 4-6
Funding allocation cascades from vision to goals, to bets, to initiatives.

Investment segmentation primarily reflects executive team judgment on how best to further the vision. Judgment is a key input in this process. Traditional investment allocation schemes are typically based on detailed ROI projections. However, when goals are transformational, allocations need to be judged on a wider set of criteria, some of which are qualitative rather than quantitative. Having good MoS and short delivery cycles helps the organization avoid investing too much in the wrong goals or bets.

Figure 4-7
Allocating funding and measures of success in the LVT.

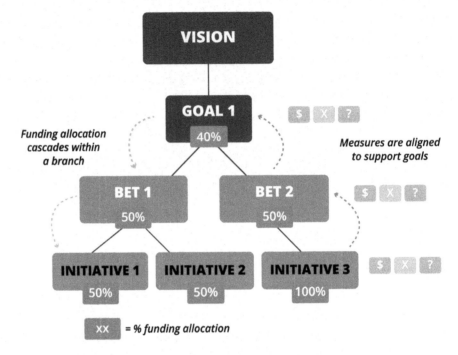

Goal and bet owners should collaborate on the budget allocation to bets and initiatives that support the goal. You'll make better budget allocation and reallocation decisions when you have clear measures that track the incremental delivery of value. This is one of the major shifts in thinking in EDGE: There's a transition from approving specific pieces of work and solutions to funding desired outcomes.

Portfolio Categorization

In large and complex portfolios, it is sometimes useful to further categorize the portfolio to maintain a balance of investment. The choice of categories depends on the specific business challenges that need to be balanced.

In our experience, it is best to keep things simple in the beginning and to resist the temptation to further categorize portfolios until there is a clear need to do so. The additional overhead required to really utilize the additional granularity is costly.

Categorization Alternatives

For those who can't resist, or who need some ideas for how they might proceed, the following examples can be considered:

- Customer type/market segment
- Three-horizons model
- Product types
- Geographic/market area

Customer Type Categorization

Customer type categories are shown in Figure 4-8. For example, in wealth management settings, customer types could be advised customers versus non-advised customers, or customer segments using demographics such as age, location, and net worth. You might also use buckets for millennials and baby boomers.

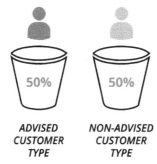

Figure 4-8
Customer type categorization example.

Three Horizon Model Categorization

McKinsey's three-horizons model[9] (shown in Figure 4-9, with the allocation shown in Figure 4-10) is designed to highlight the difference between near-term investments that expand current business operations (horizon 1) and future-focused investments that are more speculative. Horizons 2 and 3 focus on transformative business opportunities, which, though often not "urgent," are very important for long-term survival. This is one area where it is easy to compromise on future investments because returns are often in

9. For a good description of McKinsey's three-horizons model, see Baghai, Mehrdad, Steve Coley, and David White. *The Alchemy of Growth: Practical Insights for Building the Enduring Enterprise*. Reading, MA: Basic Books, 1999.

Funding Allocation   • 73 •

the future. If horizons 1 and 3 were ranked by ROI alone, there would not be any future investments in them.

Figure 4-9
Three-horizons model time frames.

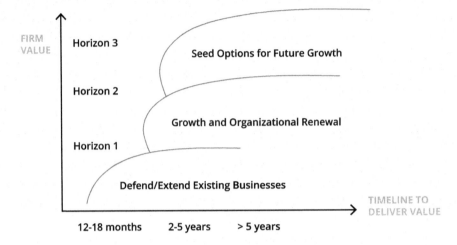

Figure 4-10
Three-horizons model investment allocation.

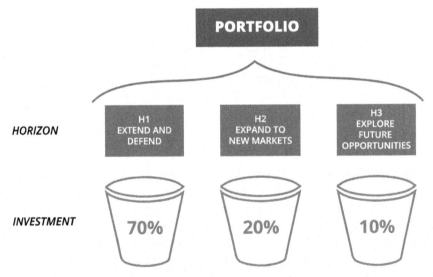

Product Life Cycle Categorization

Management literature contains a large variety of 2 × 2 matrices for evaluating products. One that has been around for a long time is the Boston Consulting Group's BCG Matrix[10] (shown in Figure 4-11, with the allocation

10. For a good description of the BCG Matrix, see Stern, Carl W., and Michael S. Deimler, eds. *The Boston Consulting Group on Strategy: Classic Concepts and New Perspectives*. 2nd ed. Hoboken, NJ: Wiley, 2006.

depicted in Figure 4-12). It is based on product life cycle theory. Other matrices may fit better in specific situations—value versus risk, for example.

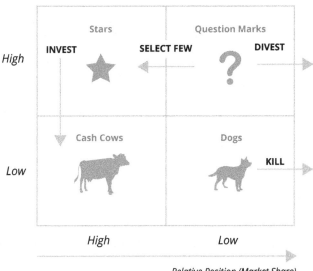

PRODUCT LIFE CYCLE CATEGORIZATION

BCG GROWTH SHARE MATRIX

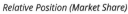

Figure 4-11
BCG Matrix for growth share.

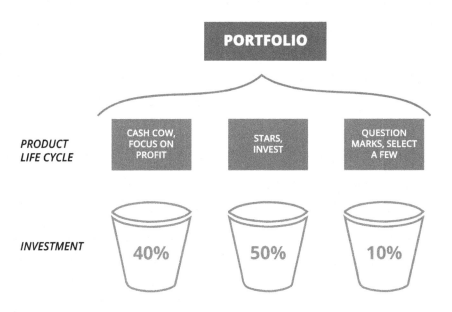

Figure 4-12
Product life cycle investment allocation.

Geographic/Market Area

Large companies may allocate investments based on their physical locations (or defined market areas (Europe, Great Britain, Asia), as shown in Figure 4-13.

Figure 4-13
Geographic investment
allocation.

Final Thoughts

The focus of this chapter was the key question, "How should we invest?" At this point, you should also be able to answer the question, "How do LVTs differ from traditional investment approaches?" Tree structures for enterprise planning have been around for decades. Management by objectives (MBO), an approach that remained popular for many years, had a vision, goal, and objective structure much like the LVT. A detailed, prioritized list of objectives was produced for each executive and manager in an organization's hierarchy. Unfortunately, a variety of problematic issues arose with MBO, the worst of which may have been the creation of a toxic environment of individualism rather than collaboration and teamwork. For example, if I had a number 1 priority objective that depended on you accomplishing a number 6 objective, that relationship often led to contention: You didn't want to work on number 6 because your performance depended not on my number 1 objective, but on your own number 1. With all the interdependencies in organizations, it was nearly impossible to untangle this web.

While not perfect, focusing on customer outcomes and customer value is more conducive to collaboration. At each level of the LVT, self-sufficient teams, rather than individuals, work on the goals, bets, and initiatives, which are themselves aligned with the desired outcome for the customer. This creates a line-of-sight to strategic intent and gives purpose to the team's work.

Using LVT correctly also means focusing on measurable customer-value outcomes, not internal measures such as ROI. Don't take this to mean that ROI isn't important—in fact, it is very important. ROI just isn't a goal, but rather a constraint. The organization has to make a profit to be a viable business. But what is the best way to make that profit? We believe it is focusing on outcomes rather than internal outputs.

Finally, implementing EDGE through LVT accepts the reality that you can't predict the future. This approach focuses on short iterations, innovation, and learning quickly so you can adapt to the reality you find there. To do this requires MoS that can be evaluated incrementally, rather than at the end of the project. Working on a small increment of value every couple of weeks supports a rapid-fire learning cycle that was not possible when projects took nine months to complete and it took even longer to determine those projects' impact on your bottom line.

Chapter 5

Measuring and Prioritizing Value

The next aspect of answering the EDGE question "How should we invest?" is developing appropriate Measures of Success (MoS). Although your Lean Value Tree (LVT) statements are outcome-oriented, you have to determine how to measure those outcomes. Without definitive MoS, you're left with flowery statements for which success or failure is arbitrary. It's one thing to establish a goal; it's quite another to identify an appropriate measure to both prioritize that goal against other investment demands and then monitor progress as initiatives move forward. Much as acceptance criteria enrich agile stories and provide critical information for developers to understand the requirements, MoS help describe the desired outcome of the work in a way that people doing the work can test to determine whether they are on track.

Why Measures Matter

Having a clear understanding of the value that the organization expects from a given portfolio of works is critical to maximizing overall value. One common misconception about measures is that they are created after the work is defined, and are used to track activity progress. Measures that are defined and articulated correctly become a powerful way to shape the work that will help achieve the desired outcome without constraining creativity.

There are three primary reasons for using MoS in EDGE:

- MoS help leadership shape and align the work, without prescribing a specific solution.
- MoS replace deliverables as the primary description of what is expected from the team doing the work.
- MoS are used throughout the delivery process to demonstrate progress, prioritize work, and support decision making on incremental funding.

Identifying Measures of Success

Ideally, MoS represent customer value—a measurement of something a customer sees as valuable (Figure 5-1). Outcomes that the organization desires, but a customer does not directly recognize as valuable, are called "benefits." The differentiation between customer value and internal business benefit is another important step in transitioning to a customer-centric view of your enterprise.

Figure 5-1
MoS should emphasize customer value as much as possible.

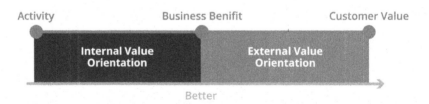

Customer Value

Customer-value MoS, such as delivery time (order to receipt) and customer satisfaction, are good measures of outcomes that represent customer value. You should strive for MoS that emphasize customer value within the available data and measurement constraints.

> **Examples of MoS That Represent Customer Value**
> - Mortgage client
>   - Original goal: Sell more mortgages
>   - Better goal: Enable more people to buy homes
>   - Measured by: Number of home purchases enabled
> - Automobile client
>   - Original goal: Reduce warranty costs
>   - Better Goal: Improve reliability for car owners
>   - Measured by: Cost of warranty repairs
> - Hotel Client
>   - Original goal: Make the hotel reception experience seamless (e.g., staff uniforms, consistent check-in)
>   - Better goal: Minimize time from taxi to pillow
>   - Measured by: Time from the moment the customer exits the vehicle to when the customer swipes the hotel key

Business Benefits

Revenue, profit, market share, and time to market are measures of benefits that are desirable to the organization, but not something a customer sees as valuable. Often benefits are useful as "guardrails" to keep the customer-focused team from giving away the store.

Activity Measures

Being on schedule, budget variance, velocity, and defect count are all examples of measures of activity that provide no directional guidance to the delivery team, and have a tenuous relationship with value. Measures of activity should be used within teams only to enable learning and continuous improvement. *Measurements of activity should never be used to evaluate goal, bet, or initiative value.*

Leading and Lagging Measures

Measures are often characterized as either leading or lagging indicators. In the context of EDGE, this is another good way to help identify useful MoS.

As an example, a MoS at the goal level that is very value-oriented—such as customer satisfaction (a lagging indicator)—might take a while to have an impact, and many different factors might influence it. It provides useful guidance at a goal level because it focuses the investment on the customer and isn't overly prescriptive of the solution. However, it's ill suited to steer initiatives because it's not very sensitive and there can be a significant delay between action and a change in the result.

Conversely, MoS for initiatives are typically leading indicators, as the examples in Figure 5-2 illustrate. These behavior-based measures are a critical source of feedback and guide decision making. They're more sensitive and therefore useful for prioritization and faster decision making—which is useful at the initiative level.

Figure 5-2

Example goal, bets, initiatives, and measures of success.

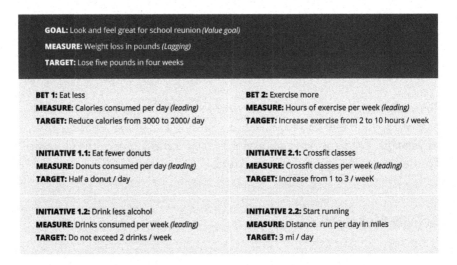

GOAL: Look and feel great for school reunion *(Value goal)*

MEASURE: Weight loss in pounds *(Lagging)*

TARGET: Lose five pounds in four weeks

BET 1: Eat less	**BET 2:** Exercise more
MEASURE: Calories consumed per day *(leading)*	**MEASURE:** Hours of exercise per week *(leading)*
TARGET: Reduce calories from 3000 to 2000/ day	**TARGET:** Increase exercise from 2 to 10 hours / week
INITIATIVE 1.1: Eat fewer donuts	**INITIATIVE 2.1:** Crossfit classes
MEASURE: Donuts consumed per day *(leading)*	**MEASURE:** Crossfit classes per week *(leading)*
TARGET: Half a donut / day	**TARGET:** Increase from 1 to 3 / weeK
INITIATIVE 1.2: Drink less alcohol	**INITIATIVE 2.2:** Start running
MEASURE: Drinks consumed per week *(leading)*	**MEASURE:** Distance run per day in miles
TARGET: Do not exceed 2 drinks / week	**TARGET:** 3 mi / day

There are certainly risks in focusing on leading indicators: You may make erroneous assumptions about the relationship between the leading indicators (inputs) and the lagging indicators (outcomes). Were that to happen, you'd be steering your initiatives with leading indicator MoS that looked good, but won't achieve your desired outcome.

Our recommendation is that you use leading indicator MoS only when you have high confidence in the correlation between those measures and customer value. If you don't have that confidence, then design some of your early activities to prove your hypothesis, before committing substantial investment. Figure 5-3 depicts how customer value, business benefit, and activity measures align on the LVT.

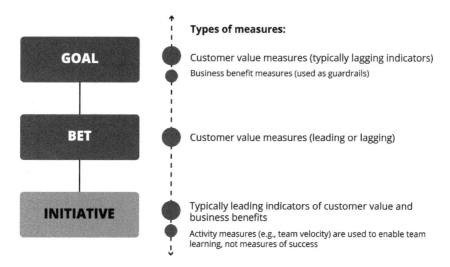

Types of measures:

Customer value measures (typically lagging indicators)
Business benefit measures (used as guardrails)

Customer value measures (leading or lagging)

Typically leading indicators of customer value and business benefits
Activity measures (e.g., team velocity) are used to enable team learning, not measures of success

Figure 5-3
How customer value, business benefit, and activity measures align on the LVT.

Number of Measures

You may need several MoS to describe the desired outcome for a portfolio (goal, bet, or initiative). Having too many MoS, however, can be counter-productive. Using a single MoS can also have undesired consequences.

For example, if you had a solitary MoS, such as customer satisfaction, it might drive satisfaction at the expense of profitability. You can avoid this undesirable outcome by adding the "guardrail" measure of profitability (a benefit), which provides the guidance that solutions should optimize customer satisfaction and profitability. Then, when your delivery team prioritizes alternative solutions, it will favor those that increase both customer satisfaction and profitability over those that impact only one of those measures.

A small set (one to three) of MoS should be crafted so that high-value options are clearly identifiable, and options that reduce value can also be recognized and avoided.

MoS that are highly correlated with each other are not helpful in the same portfolio, since by definition, if one shows positive results, so will the others. Pick the measure that's most meaningful to your team and that you can capture with the least effort.

Applying MoS to Portfolios

In EDGE, clear MoS are required for every goal, bet, and initiative. They differ in type, but it should be easy to see how MoS align and contribute to the parent as you traverse up a LVT branch, from initiative to goal.

Using MoS to Align and Differentiate Portfolios

As mentioned in Chapter 4, Building a Value-Driven Portfolio, each portfolio in the LVT should be mutually exclusive and collectively exhaustive (MECE).[1] MoS help to differentiate the portfolios within the LVT. All bets for a given goal should contribute to the MoS of the goal. At the same time, each bet should have some unique MoS or a unique effect on its parent MoS that distinguishes it from the other bets in that goal.

Similarly, MoS for initiatives should help differentiate each one from other initiatives within a bet.

1. Minto, Barbara. *The Pyramid Principle: Logic in Writing and Thinking*. 3rd ed. Harlow, UK: Prentice Hall, 2010.

Prioritizing Value

For many organizations, prioritization is extremely difficult—they want to do everything. Deciding how much to invest in existing goals versus new goals requires thought, judgment, and some luck. To reduce the risk of leading the organization down the wrong path, prioritization should be done on a regular cadence and based on customer value.

In traditional portfolio management, prioritization processes tend to focus on estimated return on investment (ROI) and on fully utilizing resources (e.g., money, people). In EDGE, an organization uses the MoS to describe the outcome it wants from each portfolio, and it uses those MoS to rank and prioritize the work in the portfolio. Prioritizing using MoS ensures an organization is working on those items that produce the maximum value.

Prioritization Approaches

Many different methods for prioritization exist. In keeping with most of our advice in EDGE, the right approach for you is the one that works. However, we would suggest the following criteria to evaluate if your approach is serving your organization well:

- Does your approach result in the highest-value portfolio item on top of your list?
- Is the effort required to accomplish the work considered so that portfolio items that have the same value contribution are sequenced with lowest effort first?
- Is there a way to incorporate other factors that affect ROI into the decision?
- Can you apply your method with the information you have available at the last responsible moment?
- Can your method be used quickly to appropriately incorporate new ideas into the prioritized list?
- Does your method produce a rank-order list (no ties)?

Relative Value Scoring

One approach to prioritizing that meets these criteria is relative value scoring. When ranking items, owners or teams don't attempt to predict the exact magnitude of the impact on MoS, only the relative impact compared to the other items in that portfolio. Owners or teams then use the same relative approach to forecast the investment or effort required to accomplish something. This approach requires a collaborative effort that leverages everyone's domain knowledge and experience to quickly make prioritization decisions. An added benefit is that it's easily adjusted as new information becomes available because this method relies on visibility, collaboration, and relative ranking.

Relative value scoring is substantially different from traditional portfolio management approaches, where great effort is expended to make some kind of upfront ROI justification. ROI is based on a series of assumptions that require validation, and shouldn't be used as the sole basis for prioritization. Doing so will constrain your ability to decide what's most valuable and to check those decisions as work is delivered and you learn.

Using a gross measurement scale such as "Low, Medium, High," or T-shirt sizes (S, M, L), or Fibonacci numbers (1, 2, 3, 5, 8, …), you utilize the wisdom of the portfolio owner team to assign a value impact score for each MoS, to each of the portfolio items. Adding up the value scores for each item and sorting this list makes the highest-value items visible, as shown in Figure 5-4. What is important in this approach is to assign scores relative to each other within the portfolio. In other words, when you are done, the items with the highest scores represent the most value relative to the other items in the list. This step gets you halfway there—you now know what is most valuable in the portfolio.

MEASURES OF SUCCESS					
Initiative	NPS	Conversion	Abandonment	Value Score	Value Priority
Idea *1	1	1	2	4	3
Idea *2	1	1	1	3	4
Idea *3	2	3	2	7	1
Idea *4	2	2	1	5	2

Figure 5-4
Value impact scoring.

Next, you need to incorporate the effort component into your scheme. By "effort," we mean the investments you will be required to make to get the value you have estimated. Effort is often expressed as money, but that doesn't have to be the only component. For example, in some situations, capacity for change can be a significant constraint and it can be useful to incorporate this factor into the effort side of the equation. Other possible Measures of Effort (MoE) are time, risk, and complexity. You can (and should) use whatever MoE help you find the lowest-effort items based on your experience. You can use the same relative scoring method employed in Figure 5-4 to assign an effort score to each item in the portfolio, total the score for each item, and sort the list as in Figure 5-5. Now you know which items will take the most effort to accomplish.

Figure 5-5

Effort impact scoring.

EFFORT IMPACT SCORE

Initiative	Investment	Risk	Change	Impact Score	Impact Priority
Idea *1	3	2	2	7	3
Idea *2	2	3	3	8	4
Idea *3	2	2	1	5	2
Idea *4	1	1	1	3	1

LOWEST IMPACT

Next, combine the two components, dividing the value score by the effort score for each item. Sorting the resulting data will sequence the portfolio items with the highest-value and lowest-effort items on top, as shown in Figure 5-6. This creates the backlog that the portfolio owner and team will manage.

Figure 5-6

Combining value and effort scoring.

Initiative	Value Score	Effort Score	V/E	Priority
Idea *1	4	7	0.57	3
Idea *2	3	8	0.38	4
Idea *3	7	5	1.40	2
Idea *4	5	3	1.67	1

**HIGHEST VALUE
FOR LOWEST EFFORT**

One word of caution here: You want to keep your MoS and MoE scheme as simple as possible. It's important that you can very quickly assign scores based on the wisdom of the team without significant delays for analysis.

Cost of Delay

A more sophisticated way of prioritizing portfolio items is to use Cost of Delay (CoD).[2] Fundamentally, CoD is the value of having the desired work completed earlier. Typically it is expressed as the monetary value of a one-month change in receiving the work. For example, if a new software feature is expected to improve the customer experience in such a way that it would have a positive impact on your customer retention rate (a MoS for the portfolio),

2. See Don Reinertsen's book for a complete description of CoD. Reinertsen, Donald G. *The Principles of Product Development Flow: Second Generation Lean Product Development*. Redondo Beach, CA: Celeritas Publishing, 2009.

you would use the monetary value of that change in customer retention for one month as the CoD for the feature. The assumption is that if you delayed the implementation of that feature for one month, you would not get the benefit of that positive impact on customer retention.

In this example, you can see that you need to have a good understanding of the relationship between your feature and its impact on customer retention. Similar understanding is required for every item in your portfolio to be useful for prioritization. For mature portfolios with delivery teams that deeply understand their portfolio domain and have the necessary infrastructure to capture and analyze their MoS data, this might be possible. In our experience with some of the world's largest organizations, however, this level of sophistication is usually far beyond their current capabilities. For a really good description of the effort involved in implementing CoD for portfolio prioritization, see Blackswan Farming's white paper[3] on their experience with Maersk.

For the sake of completeness, let's finish our example of applying CoD for prioritization. In the example, CoD is used to represent the value of the feature. This replaces the relative value MoS score used in the earlier example. To complete the equation, we bring the measure of effort concept into the picture. This step allows us to identify the most valuable features that require the least effort to deliver. This method is usually referred to as Cost of Delay divided by duration (CD3).[4] To finish the prioritization, divide the CoD by the duration to deliver the feature and get a numeric score that can be ranked as shown in Figure 5-6. This method is irresistible to organizations that like the precision of its calculations.

Our experience suggests some additional cautions are warranted. Besides requiring deep understanding of the relationship between your candidate work and your desired outcome, CD3 strictly focuses on duration, as the entire scheme hinges on utilizing constrained resources to deliver maximum value. For a technology organization that is myopically focused on getting maximum efficiency out of the resources with which it has been entrusted, this is a very effective method. However, EDGE suggests that you should focus on actual value realized—and that involves far more than

3. Arnold, Joshua, and Özlem Yüce. "Experience Report: Maersk Line" Black Swan Farming [blog], 2013. http://blackswanfarming.com/experience-report-maersk-line/.
4. Reinertsen, Donald G. *The Principles of Product Development Flow: Second Generation Lean Product Development.* Redondo Beach, CA: Celeritas Publishing, 2009.

the technology organization delivering its work. Indeed, the entire value stream must operate in concert to deliver that value.

With CD3, the duration component does not provide the opportunity to consider other types of effort, as described earlier. For example, we have seen portfolios where the change management effort required for implementation was a more significant constraint than the duration. Reputational risk is another factor that can drive prioritization decisions in a more significant way than the time it would take, or the cost associated with the development of the technology. Certainly, there are ways to incorporate these concerns into a CD3 base prioritization scheme. However, we believe this level of sophistication is beyond many teams, and therefore this approach could create a trap that gives the appearance of precision, but has unintended consequences.

Our advice is to start with relative value scoring. Then, when you have a well-functioning process that needs further improvement, consider experimenting with CD3 in some of your highly dynamic portfolios.

Managing the Strategic Backlog

Businesses always have more ideas than they have had capacity to investigate those ideas. So, as you construct your LVT, you'll likely end up with things that are not yet funded and may be backlog candidates. As you deliver on initiatives, you'll also gather ideas by learning what helps the business and what hurts it. As always, your competition and the market won't stand still; thus, new ideas will be generated to address new developments as the market changes.

One benefit of having the entire organization aligned and more familiar with the investment profile through the LVT is that many new ideas will emerge—sometimes from unexpected places. This is a good thing, but such growth needs to be managed so you don't end up overwhelmed. The VRT helps with this by collecting all of the ideas in a pool of potential backlog items. In some organizations, we call this unvetted pool the "inbox."

The VRT also schedules regular reviews of potential ideas to prioritize them for grooming and possible inclusion in the backlog of bets or initiatives. The intention is to maintain a small, healthy, and well-vetted backlog of ideas that could be taken on for work as capacity frees up.

Prioritization Challenges

For long-lived delivery teams, initiative backlogs[5] must include sustaining (break–fix) and tech-debt items in addition to new work. The sources of these items will vary depending on the organization. Common ones are service desks, incident ticket systems, and field support. It is the portfolio owners' responsibility (with the VRT's help) to ensure that all sources of potential work are fed into an integrated backlog of work to be considered. There can be no "back door" into the system. All these types of work are prioritized using the same ranking framework as new ideas.

Work intake is straightforward once the LVT and the MoS have been established and the prioritization mechanism is in place. Since the highest-priority items are always at the top of the backlog, new work can be taken on when capacity is freed up.

Ruthless Prioritization

During our work with a telecommunications organization, we found the organization was notorious for starting new work without limiting the amount of work in progress. Beyond the mechanical process of visualizing all work in flight, the discipline of prioritizing new work wasn't considered. This led to multiple backlogs, where the same team was simultaneously working on a bunch of equally important priorities, promised to multiple stakeholders.

As we started to embed the discipline and mindset shift to ruthlessly prioritize all potential work, the organization became comfortable asking tough questions about priorities. For example, during sprint planning, a product owner introduced a new piece of work that required immediate attention. A developer pointed to the LVT on the wall and asked, "How does this new work align to our goals?" It didn't. And the work was prioritized out of the team's backlog for possible future review.

---

5. For more about integrated backlogs, see Chapter 7, Integrating Strategic and Business as Usual Portfolios.

Final Thoughts

Prioritizing in this way often runs counter to the culture of large organizations, which typically desire precision in their estimating processes that feed prioritization. Cost/benefit analysis that produces ROI calculations provides a level of comfort to decision makers who are faced with comparing complex and costly investments.

In our experience, most organizations become good at predicting only what they have extensive experience in. They're able to use the data they have accumulated and the consistency of their process to create accurate statistical predictions.

Unfortunately, when you're searching for customer value in a highly dynamic and competitive marketplace, you never have that experience. You are pioneering—searching for new sources of value and routes to get there. If you apply estimation methods that rely heavily on data to drive your prioritization process, then that process will likely slow down as you attempt to gather the data you need. Your value stream will be constantly changing as you attempt to optimize your results. Both of these factors will conspire to make your attempts at statistical estimation futile.

As an alternative, we've proposed a method of prioritizing that emphasizes speed rather than precision. Speed enables you to get to the learning as quickly as possible, rather than remaining in "analysis paralysis." The relative value scoring method described in this chapter relies on the collective wisdom of your team to weigh the data you do have, the team's experience in the domain, and their own value-creating capability in an attempt to discern the relative differences in value and effort within their portfolio. Team members can't tell you exactly how much value you'll get from a particular investment, but they can tell you whether you are likely to get the most value from one particular investment versus another.

Applying this approach to prioritization requires the components of EDGE to be in place: long-lived teams that have deep domain knowledge and have had the opportunity to optimize their ways of working to be consistent. The traditional program/project operating model is missing several of the key ingredients that make this approach successful. For example, in a traditional project-based operating model, teams tend to be short-lived, and assigned to work based on availability. Because they change domains frequently, they don't have the opportunity to learn about the domain they're working within. They also don't have the opportunity to optimize their work process because the team members are changing frequently. In EDGE, we advocate that those teams stay focused on a particular domain for a longer period of time.[6] This affords team members the opportunity to learn deeply about what creates value in that domain and the opportunity to optimize their way of working and become more consistent.

As you can see, this approach relies heavily on the people in the system. It requires investing in their learning and developing trust within the culture. For some organizations, that may be a substantial undertaking, but one we believe can produce a substantial ROI.

6. See Chapter 9, Autonomous Teams and Collaborative Decision Making.

Chapter 6

Building a Product Mindset

Products are the vehicles that deliver value to customers. Turning an initiative into an innovative product that evolves over time requires a product mindset that stresses delivering customer value in the present and adaptability for the future.

Product people encourage teams to deliver a *continuous* stream of value over time—a balancing act that pushes team members to make good decisions. Considering a continuous stream of value helps prioritize both current and future investments. It means that you want your product release 5 to be as effective and efficient as release 1. A product mindset needs to be adaptive and responsive, as exemplified by the use of hypothesis testing with rapid feedback described in this chapter.

EDGE is an operating model that helps all the parts of an organization move away from focusing on features and being output driven, and toward solving customer problems and being value (outcome) focused. For organizations to realize value from their investments, delivery teams need the ability to take the strategic direction (from the Lean Value Tree [LVT]) and articulate how they intend to deliver value to the customer, then apply a hypothesis and learning approach with clear measures of success to drive incremental decisions as the product evolves.

An important shift in thinking is the belief that no one can predict exactly what will be successful in the marketplace. Hence, applying a "test and learn" experimentation approach is crucial in investing and building the right things. This experimentation approach assumes ideas that don't exist in the market today are not proven (or just because a competitor has proven the idea, that does not mean the idea will be successful for your organization), so that there is a hypothesis of value associated with them. These hypotheses form the basis of how teams approach the process of slicing up potential ideas for incremental testing and validation in the market. One of the benefits of breaking down products into a hypothesis framework is that this approach allows incremental steering and internal feedback between the people delivering the work (delivery teams) and the leaders (portfolio owners and stakeholders) responsible for the eventual realization of business benefits.

Moving from Projects to Products

To enable product thinking, there must be a shift from the traditional ways of *delivering a project* to *evolving a product*, as depicted in Figure 6-1. The key difference between a project and a product is that products have a customer and expected value. This definition of product focuses the delivery team on the value they are delivering.

Figure 6-1
Project versus product mindset.

PROJECT MINDSET	PRODUCT MINDSET
Temporary teams	Long-lived teams
Build-once mentality	Test and learn mentality
Customer feedback at the end	Customer feedback throughout the product
Release once	Release continuously
Success is measured by delivery of scope within time and budget	Success is measured by customer satisfaction and value created
Scope is determined by stakeholders	Scope guidelines are set with stakeholders and teams learn through experimentation and customer feedback

Projects typically consist of a collection of features implemented within a timeframe. A project team is temporarily assembled to complete the set of features within that time frame. When the defined work is complete, the team is disbanded. This process creates several constraints on maximizing value for the customer. First, the temporary nature of projects causes stakeholders to include features that *might* be needed (known as "feature bloat") because there is a set window of time and budget allocated. Second, this temporary project mindset assumes that the market environment will not continue to change or evolve, and once the project is complete, there is no need to continue investment. This leads to missed opportunities to improve and evolve the product, and eventually wasted effort, as teams hurry to build a list of features yet to be validated by customers. Third, ownership of realized value is in the hands of the stakeholder team that handed the list of features to the delivery team. Because stakeholders have an urgency and expectation of a list of features to be delivered, teams often have little visibility into the reasons and assumptions that led to the inclusion of those features on the list, and they lose sight of the customer as they march toward building the features within the time frame allocated.

In contrast, a product belongs to a delivery team that owns all aspects of the product—from new ideas for product expansion to the support and maintenance of the product. The realization of expected value, and therefore the details of what gets built, are the responsibility of the delivery team. The stakeholders are responsible for articulating the expected value and enabling a team to explore potential solutions. The delivery team does not disband (in the way teams in projects spin up and disband), but rather stays together throughout the duration of the product's life, until the organization decides to redirect investment or sunset the product. These empowered teams must make prioritization decisions that affect both the current support of the product and the future direction of the product. They are responsible for the end-to-end customer experience of the total product, from a new customer signing up to an existing customer leaving the product. This perspective represents an important mindset shift for organizations aspiring to create team autonomy and accountability of the end-to-end customer experience.

While this paradigm shift has important organizational structure and design implications, the emphasis in this chapter is on why the product mindset is important in delivering a value-driven portfolio.

Waking Up the Sleeping Bear

We were working with a health organization to shape its customer engagement and product rationalization strategy.

For many years, teams within the organization were separated into "support and maintenance" of existing products and "new-product innovation." The support and maintenance teams grew in size and complexity over time as the number of unique products they had to support and maintain also grew. The new-product innovation teams expanded and contracted based on the amount of investment available to launch new products. One of the common complaints from the new-product innovation teams was that they never went beyond delivering the minimum viable product (MVP) before they had to hand over a suboptimal product to the support and maintenance team. The support and maintenance team had a backlog of customer feature requests so long that customers complained about waiting more than two years before they could see basic improvements in the product.

In addition, collaboration between the two teams was difficult, because the overhead needed to transition knowledge was ineffective, making initial production support frustrating for the customer.

As time progressed, very limited data were collected about customer usage of existing products. As a result, product rationalization was nearly impossible to do. As products matured through the product life cycle, the organization experienced a diminishing return on value of those legacy products. The organization had no idea how many active customers were using the products. And they couldn't make contact with customers because it might alert them to the realization that they were paying for a product they weren't using! This dilemma was called "waking up the sleeping bear" and it's a common problem we've observed in organizations that haven't shifted from delivering projects to adopting a product mindset, particularly with subscription-based business models.

The Role of Product People in Organizations

As organizations face pressure to deliver faster in today's hypercompetitive market, the role of product people has become increasingly critical. The expectation is that the product will be the connector between what customers value and the realization of business benefits. This role becomes the glue between portfolio owners' assumptions and the teams responsible for validating those assumptions in the pursuit of delivering value to customers.

Important Product Skills

The expectations of a product person's skills have grown in breadth and depth, to the point that they are actually too much for one person to feasibly have! Product thinking is best represented in the skills outlined in the following list, rather than by job title. Various titles may be given to people with a product mindset—product manager, product owner, product strategist, and so on. In fact, some of the best product thinkers don't have "product" in their title at all. The point is to focus less on what title these people carry, and more on whether they have the skills to enable the alignment and delivery of value. In this section we explore the most important product skills needed for defining and delivering customer value.

- *Creator and champion of the vision.* The product person works closely with stakeholders to understand the business direction and shapes a vision for how the product might help the organization deliver on the strategy.
- *Builds organizational alignment of the vision and direction.* The product person aligns the delivery team to the organizational goals. It's easy for teams to lose sight of why they are building something. Defining organizational goals with portfolio teams and aligning the goals to the products being built keeps teams on track to always be delivering value.

- *Embodies coaching and not gatekeeping.* A self-sufficient team (see Chapter 9, Autonomous Teams and Collaborative Decision Making) should be empowered to make their own decisions as a team and to contribute their unique perspectives of the problem. Effective product leadership is not about controlling or telling teams what to build. Instead, it allows unique perspectives from individuals to be considered, and enables different ways of solving problems to take flight. The team needs to be inspired, and the product person acts like a team coach to enable the whole team to be successful.
- *Advocate for the customer.* Product people believe in the value proposition because it will deliver something that customers will love (and they were responsible for defining the value to customers). They understand users' pains and delights, and use this understanding to make informed, forward-thinking decisions. If product people are out of touch with the customers' needs, they cannot brilliantly orchestrate product delivery or successfully align stakeholders and portfolio owners on the value of the investment in the product.
- *Keeper of the process and evangelist for the product mindset.* Product thinking involves using Measures of Success (MoS) to guide teams toward making sound decisions that focus on value. A good process enables teams to think and act creatively, rather than emphasizing throughput and features delivered—which are both measures of activity, but don't always translate into value. As hypotheses get validated throughout the product development process, the product person choreographs when to bring in data for Periodic Value Review to effectively seek additional funding or make suggestions to kill or pivot on a product idea.
- *Thinks beyond the immediate MVP to set a direction for the product.* The product person facilitates organizational understanding of the current focus of investment and the promised value, while articulating the future needs of the product and hypotheses of value. This individual is responsible for shaping the definition of what an MVP could be by using information, data, and insights. The product person continuously validates the MVP assumptions and shares this with portfolio team and delivery teams, balancing tactical immediate needs while setting the future direction of the product.

- *Translates customer needs into requirements and facilitates building the product backlog.* Defining and slicing the requirements so that work can be prioritized at a more granular level is an important skill in the delivery of value. There will always be instances where lower-value options could be selected for development. It is a product person's responsibility to help the team decide which components are the most valuable, even at the most granular levels, so that development effort is not wasted on lower-value items that customers will take a neutral attitude toward. For example, if you were building a customer dashboard (user interface) for interpreting data, you could introduce the ability to sort, filter, search, and generate a report on the data. If the highest value is the sort function, it is the product person's responsibility to define and prioritize that first, and to suggest that the other functions be built later when further customer feedback is collected.

Product and Portfolio Team Collaboration

The interaction between portfolio teams and delivery teams is an important and often overlooked component for organizations wanting to evolve the way they work to maximize the value delivered to customers. Feedback loops must exist between portfolio owners, who make assumptions of possible value, and the delivery teams, which are responsible for delivering the assumed value. This is a different way of working than traditional approaches because you are not asking stakeholders to feed teams a features (or solutions) list, but to empower teams to solve a customer problem or need and come up with a solution that has been validated with customers.

To enable this new way of working, the role of product has become a key part of the puzzle. When they fail to embrace product thinking, organizations experience frustration, as teams are disconnected from the customer problem or value desired, products get implemented with low customer adoption, and very little value is realized from investments.

In traditional waterfall organizations, alignment of work is clear because work trickles down to teams in the form of product ideas, preset solutions, and a fixed features list. As some organizations move to more autonomous teams and agile practices, the link can be lost between executives' desired customer value and the delivery of the work. The autonomous team relies heavily on the role of product as the "glue" that brings diverse perspectives together and aligns them with the portfolio team and customer expectations. As described in Chapter 8, Lightweight Governance, EDGE provides a framework for how to bridge this gap between expected value and realized value.

Defining Products and the Connection to the LVT

This section focuses on how work is further broken down from the LVT to product blueprints, and then how product blueprints connect to agile product backlogs. These frameworks (see Figures 6-2 and 6-3) become the backbone for creating flow and alignment from executive leadership strategic intent to the teams that deliver value to customers.

Figure 6-2

Creating flow and alignment between strategy and execution: from LVT to product blueprint to agile product backlog.

BREAKING DOWN THE PORTFOLIO

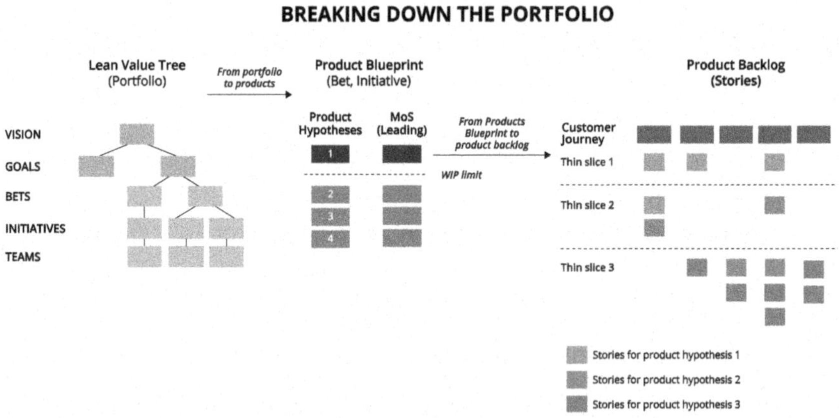

Figure 6-3

Breaking down work from portfolio to bets and initiatives in the product blueprint to agile product backlogs.

BUILDING A PRODUCT MINDSET

How Products Are Derived from the LVT

Not all bets and initiatives start off as well-defined products in the LVT. When a bet or initiative is first defined, it comes with many assumptions about the expected value. This section describes two possible ways that a product would exist in the LVT: as a new product that doesn't exist today (i.e., an initiative in the LVT) or as potential product enhancement to an existing product.

Initiatives and Products

Not all initiatives are products. For new products that don't exist in the current portfolio of products offered by the organization, a product will be an initiative as defined in the LVT. Where the product exists (and a product team is assigned to actively support the existing customers of the product), initiatives are defined as potential ways you might implement a bet (from Chapter 4, Building a Value-Driven Portfolio). That implementation could be a business initiative, a technical product, or a service. A bet is a hypothesis of value and initiatives are a way of testing the hypothesis. Developing hypotheses helps focus development effort on the most important questions to answer early.

For example, for a retail organization, one of its bets was defined as follows:

Bet: *Give me access to the best garments where I am, when I want it.*

To achieve this bet for the customer, two initiatives were identified:

Initiative 1: Empower employees to have the best buying power. Presently, the business process for approvals is lengthy and cumbersome, which results in suboptimal buying power for employees to source the best garments in the market. This initiative is a business process reengineering effort (not product) to streamline and simplify the steps needed for approvals.

Initiative 2: Provide the best tools for employees to discover and source the best garments. Presently, the current suite of systems to locate garments involves different disparate systems that don't always show the ideal garment matches. This initiative is to build a product that would optimize the entire experience for sourcing garments for the sourcing team (i.e., the customers/users of the product).

This next section focuses on the scenario where initiatives are products.

Bets and Products

A well-framed bet (with clear measures of success) should spark a number of possible product ideas. When kicking off a new product, we find it extremely beneficial to get started by holding a discovery workshop with the bet owner, product person, stakeholders, and delivery team assigned to the initiative.

The goals of a discovery workshop are to create a shared understanding of the bet and how the product will achieve the bet and to co-create a path forward for the team. The discovery workshop marks the beginning of a relationship and ongoing dialogue between the delivery team assigned to the initiative team and the portfolio team. Periodic Value Review (see Chapter 8, Lightweight Governance) is the regular cadence for this dialogue as the product evolves throughout the life cycle.

A discovery workshop should include the following things:

- Rationale for the goal, bet, or initiative
- Supporting evidence of the market opportunity
- Landscape/competitor analysis
- Financial assumptions
- Organizational analysis (e.g., strengths, weaknesses, brand considerations)
- Validation of fundamental assumptions that are likely to change product direction (through research, data, or quantitative or qualitative feedback)
- Ideation of potential ideas and ways to achieve the outcome
- Hypotheses identification for future validation
- Defined measures of success

Breaking Down Bets into Products

Breaking down a bet will determine the definition of the product. Since bets are hypotheses of value and frame the alternative directions for achieving the goal, bets should not specify a product solution. Instead, they should describe the intended approach toward the goal. In our financial services example, one of the important strategic goals was as follows:

Goal: To be the market leader in retirement solutions, as measured by market share.

The firm saw two potential bets that it could place to meet this goal:

Bet 1: Increase market share by earning all the customer's business across banking and wealth. The organization believed this bet had potential to help it achieve the goal because data revealed it had low market share of customers in the baby boomer segment who held both banking and wealth products with one financial institution. Its existing customers were holding products at other financial institutions.

Bet 2: Help the baby boomer segment throughout their entire retirement journey. The firm believed this bet had potential to help it achieve the goal because initial qualitative research revealed the needs of this segment of customers were changing rapidly during this life stage. This segment had unique qualities that differed from those of previously targeted segments, as boomers were "redefining retirement" compared to the previous generation. Boomers didn't want to look to the previous generation (their parents) to define their retirement journey (which looked like stopping work at age 65 and spending as little money as possible to ensure they had enough money to make it through their last years). Instead, boomers were going back to school, changing careers, and moving into consulting part-time. They sought advice from friends and people going through a similar phase in their life. The current products in the market, and existing financial advice models, catered to the previous generation—instilling fear of sickness and running out of money—rather than focusing on how retirees could achieve the things they wanted with a solid financial plan to support a much longer retirement journey horizon.

From the definition of these bets, the discovery workshop focused on a cross-functional team ideation exercise to come up with potential product hypotheses of value. The results are shown in Figures 6-4 and 6-5.

Figure 6-4

Example of product within LVT (measures and targets omitted for simplicity).

VISION	Be the most trusted investment solutions provider
GOAL	Be the market leader of retirement solutions
BET 1	Help baby boomers through their entire retirement journey
INITIATIVE	A different financial advice model for boomers segment (product)
PRODUCT HYPOTHESES	We believe that by providing low-cost advice to people prior to retirement (5–7 years out), we can help customers better achieve their retirement goals. We will validate this idea by introducing a specialist advisor, who is not branded as a "retirement advisor," but rather specializes in retirement advice.

Figure 6-5

Example of a consumer platform and product within LVT (measures and targets omitted for simplicity).

VISION	Be the most trusted investment solutions provider
GOAL	Be the market leader of retirement solutions
BET 2	Earn all of our customers' business (banking and wealth)
INITIATIVE	Integrated banking and 401(k) experience (assume financial products remain the same)
PRODUCT HYPOTHESES	**Hypothesis 1 (validate first)** We believe that by being able to see my 401k and banking product balances in one place will result in more awareness of 401(k) investments (reduced apathy) which we will measure through feedback from prototypes of the experience. **Hypothesis 2 (validate next)** We believe that providing an online rollover of 401(k) service will result in consolidation of 401(k) investments, which we will measure by adding a sign-up button in the authenticated banking page and tracking sign-ups.

Defining the Product

There is a common myth in the agile community that if we are "agile," then we don't need to plan up front. Conceptually, a lot of upfront planning can incur waste (as demonstrated with traditional waterfall ways of working). Even so, looking into the future reduces the risk of building the wrong thing or going too far in a direction you didn't want to go. A product blueprint is less a detailed plan or detailed definition of the product, and more a high-level map that guides teams in a direction. It is not a detailed step-by-step plan of how to get there.

Deciding "how much" product definition is necessary isn't always easy. Here are some guidelines to determine whether you have enough to move forward:

- Have you identified the key hypotheses that, if invalidated, would cause a change in direction for the product? Are you comfortable in moving forward while knowing these hypotheses will need to be validated?
- Are the outstanding hypotheses well communicated, visible, and understood among the stakeholder group and delivery team?
- Do they understand what is needed to validate each hypothesis, including the timing, impact, and potential changes in direction?
- Are the appropriate risks and dependencies communicated?
- Consider timeboxed planning to avoid going too far in a particular direction.

Core Elements of a Product Blueprint

Information conveyed in a product blueprint can vary depending on the type of product and where it is in the product life cycle. At a minimum, the product blueprint should clearly articulate the following elements.

Alignment to Organizational Goals on the LVT

Clearly describe why this is important to the organization and provide a clear mapping to the LVT. There should be articulation of how this product fits within the broader business and technical context of the organization.

Elevator Pitch

An elevator pitch is a concise overview of which problem the product solves and how it creates value in the marketplace.

Key Measures of Success

The product blueprint should contain customer metrics that describe the success of the product (e.g., new customer sign-ups, positive customer reviews) as well as the desired business benefits from this initiative (e.g., revenue). Identify the key drivers in the market or within the organization that make it urgent to make this product investment. Explain why the investment should be done now, and why the organization is uniquely positioned to take advantage of this market opportunity.

Hypotheses Validated or to Be Validated

Hypotheses are assumptions about the product that have either been validated or are still to be validated. It is good practice to have a history of the key product decisions made over time, what's been proven or disproven, and key learnings. Sharing customer quotes from research and testing sessions in this context helps people understand why key decisions were made and builds customer empathy.

> *"We have guesses about what's good for the user, but we're mostly wrong. No matter how good you are, you're mostly wrong."*
>
> —Adam Pisoni, CTO of Yammer

Target Customers and Their Needs

Typically, there are multiple customers for the product. A product blueprint describes who the customers are and why the product is needed by these customers. There should also be a description of which customer segments exist and who the early adopters might be.

Customer Goals

Customer goals represent a desired customer outcome. A customer goal has a series of steps required to complete the goal. For example, if the product you are building is Google Maps, you might have the following customer goals:

- Discover the optimum driving route to get from A to B.
- Discover the optimum route from A to B using public transportation.
- Discover restaurants near me.

Customer Journeys

Customer journeys describe an end-to-end customer experience. The reason we use customer journeys instead of a list of features is because customer journeys go beyond the digital product to describe the customer's context, the way that the customer uses the product, additional products and services needed to complete the goal, and the interactions with people involved in the experience.

Customer journeys are also crucial for prioritizing valuable thin slices to release to customers. Typically, agile user stories (requirements) are mapped to the user journey to show how the requirement will help complete a customer journey.

Prototypes That Bring the Product Vision to Life

A prototype can be anything from a whiteboard sketch to a digital mockup of the experience to an early build of the product. The intent in creating the prototype is to spend as little time and energy as needed to prove or disprove a hypothesis through customer testing. Prototypes bring together the vision of the product and help draw out assumptions that people have about the product. This is especially helpful in the early stages of defining a product idea, but prototypes also help describe future enhancements to the product that haven't yet been built.

Many types of prototypes can help bring the product vision to life. Some of the most effective and low-cost ones include a product page website, product box activity, a physical prototype for users to interact with (made of foam core and Play-Doh), and user journey sketches on a storyboard. For more ideas and tips for creating prototypes to get feedback, the following books are great resources:

- *This Is Service Design Methods*, by Marc Stickdorn et al.
- *The Lean Product Guide*, by Linda Luu
- *The Lean Product Playbook*, by Dan Olsen

Competitive Advantage

Competitive advantage is the articulation of the competitive advantage that the organization will receive from investing in this product. It includes the articulation of the current-state competitor landscape, and how it will change with the release of this product into the market.

Customer Adoption Plan

A customer adoption plan describes the customers who have been identified as early adopters of the product, as well as the potential sequencing of customer groups that will be participating in feedback sessions or have agreed to be part of pilot releases.

What a Product Blueprint Is and Is Not

This section clarifies what a product blueprint is or is not.

A Product Blueprint Is a Communication Tool

A product blueprint is a communication tool to help align the organization and create a shared understanding of the future direction of the product. The consumers of a product blueprint and their purpose in understanding the information in a blueprint are outlined here:

- Stakeholders who need to understand how future investments in the product could contribute to achieving strategic goals
- The Value Realization Team (VRT), to enable macro-level resource planning, investment allocation, and change management activities
- Product teams, to manage dependencies, sequencing, release planning, technical decisions, and architectural considerations
- Product owners, to share product decisions and hypotheses validated through research, and future assumptions about the product
- Portfolio owners, to prioritize investments based on relative value

- Sales teams, to manage customer relationships, particularly in business-to-business (B2B) products where future releases of the product are an important negotiation tool for contract renewals
- Customer research teams, to assist with planning different types of research needs and recruiting customers
- Human resources, for capability investments and addressing near-term gaps in hiring and selection

It's Not a Detailed Plan, Agile Product Backlog, or Product Roadmap

An agile product backlog is a prioritized list of all requirements that need to be worked on by the delivery team, typically broken down into smaller chunks known as stories. Such backlogs are an effective way of helping the delivery team manage and communicate all the work that needs to be done and enable value to be released incrementally in a way that is usable for customers. The problem with relying on agile product backlogs as a communication tool for portfolio teams and stakeholders is that they don't describe the compelling experience you are creating for your customers and the unique value proposition that will inspire customers to buy your product or continuously pay for your product.

Linda was coaching a product team that had been practicing agile development for a year. They had stories defined, prioritized into two-week iterations, and a backlog that was visible to anyone who visited the team space or was working in another location through the project software tracking tool Jira. Despite all this visibility, the CEO and the product owner often disagreed about the future direction of the product. Why did this happen? Because the organization used a granular product backlog as the basis for discussion. Product backlogs are typically at a feature/story level and are primarily intended to help the team to align and prioritize near-term work. But they don't do a good job of creating a line-of-sight to the "why" behind the work. For this reason, product backlogs are not appropriate for an executive or stakeholder audience, whereas a bet backlog would be appropriate.

"Product blueprint" is not another name for "product roadmap." Product roadmaps give in to the temptation to create a sequence of features that have dates committed to them. A list of features prioritized into a sequence is no better than a list of features: It does not communicate the value of the product to customers and business.

A Product Blueprint Is Never Static

In our experience, as soon as a product blueprint is made available, it is ripe for change. As a communication tool, it should be readily open to feedback and evolution. A product blueprint should be a living document, ideally displayed near the product team space on a large wall and described on cards that can be moved around. This method enables people to have a conversation at the wall, bring new ideas to be tested, and communicate with anyone who is either a consumer of or contributor to the product blueprint. While the product person is ultimately accountable for curating and maintaining the product blueprint, it is also the product person's responsibility to orchestrate alignment on the product vision and priorities, obtaining feedback from the diverse needs of different stakeholder groups and always focusing on the ultimate value that the product will provide.

A Product Blueprint Should Not Be the Mechanism to Hold Product Teams Accountable

While we shy away from attaching dates to high-level items on the product blueprint that are far into the future, sometimes it is a necessary lens that is needed for organizational planning. In an instance where dates are highly visible, the product blueprint should not be the mechanism used to hold product teams accountable. Rather, dates into the future should be used as a guideline, and the release plans should be a better indication of when customers will receive the product updates. Team should be held accountable to delivering value to the customer, as described in the measures section of this book (see Chapter 5, Measuring and Prioritizing Value).

Visualizing and Communicating Product Blueprints

There are many ways to visualize a product blueprint and articulate the information represented in a product blueprint. In terms of format, visual tools such as PowerPoint presentations, physical prototypes, wireframe mockups, and customer storyboards are the most effective.

Deciding on the best visualization depends on the type of product, your vision for the product, the audience, your communication preferences, and geographic proximity. We encourage teams to experiment with different methods to discover the most effective means.

We've also found regular showcases (generally fortnightly or monthly) to be helpful. In these forums, stakeholders and people not in the immediate delivery team are invited to an informal walkthrough of the product progress, key decisions made, and customer feedback. This method focuses on the results of the experiments that feed decisions, invites fast feedback, and encourages ideas and co-creation of the future product priorities. It also helps remove any surprises of scope or expectations during the product evolution.

Creating Agile Product Backlogs

This section address the process of further breaking down the LVT from products to an agile product backlog, which sets up the delivery team to begin implementation and further validation of hypotheses. One of the key benefits of further breaking down a product into a backlog of work is that it empowers teams to prioritize based on customer value, not plan too far ahead, and solicit incremental feedback from customers as well as internal stakeholders and the portfolio team. This incremental approach to delivery allows the organization to realize value sooner, as the customer doesn't have to wait for a "full-featured" dashboard, for example, to start using the data to make decisions. Thus, the organization can realize benefits (such as increased sales or conversions) earlier with a lower initial investment. This product evolution can become self-funding, with additional investments in the product ramping up as return on investment is incrementally proven earlier.

Why MVP Is Just a Starting Conversation

> *"A Minimum Viable Product is the smallest thing you can build that delivers customer value (and as a bonus captures some of that value back)."*
>
> —Ash Maurya

When coaching teams, we often see a team engaging in lengthy debates about what the MVP of a product should be. One of the problems is the *viable* part of the MVP definition—it is often assumed to mean *commercially* viable. At the time of defining the MVP, you are likely to have more hypotheses untested than tested. In turn, spending lots of time up front defining a viable product is usually just wasted effort.

One of the big traps that teams fall into when trying to define the MVP is feature bloat (functions of the product, such as ability to print a report) and the temptation to cover every single edge case of the product (e.g., save a report, modify a report, share a report) rather than the smallest piece of customer value (Is that report even useful?) that will enable us to test our most important hypotheses. This is typically caused by accepting these MVP myths as unassailable truths:

- We cannot release an incomplete product, because our customers will be confused and we will lose our reputation and taint our brand. So *all* these features need to be in the MVP before we release something.
- After the MVP is launched, the organization stops funding, we celebrate, and then we move on to the next shiny thing. Therefore, we need to fit as many features into the MVP as possible, because we have only one shot.
- We do "fat MVPs" around here, so it's okay to add more than what's considered "the smallest thing."
- Our customers don't understand the MVP concept, so we must go with "big bang" releases.
- It takes too long to train staff, so we're better off releasing once and making it "complete."
- We need to do a lot of quantitative testing to know for sure that this will work.

These problems can be avoided by thin slicing the product into a series of valuable experiences for the customer. Making the pieces of the product even smaller than the MVP and applying a rapid test-and-learn approach (with clear measures of success) alleviates the preceding concerns, as portfolio teams gain visibility and early learnings to help them make better decisions about potential product investments. Likewise, delivery teams gain confidence that they are headed in the right direction as they apply an iterative approach to building and "checking in" with customers. This thin slicing approach to product is described next.

Thin Slicing: An Alternative Approach to MVP

An alternative to using MVP is defining work in thin slices of value. A thin slice is typically smaller than the definition of MVP (there are many thin slices within an MVP) and is released to a smaller subset of customers as an early pilot. A thin slice of the product is prioritized to facilitate maximum team learning. Thin slices are typically framed as hypotheses, and the definition of a thin slice could be as small as a front-end-only prototype to assist with contextual feedback sessions, or some basic data visualizations for a data-heavy product to validate which data or insights are most useful to the user. The focus is on learning, and the product could shift in a different direction depending on the outcome of that learning.

Thin slices are made up of stories (a more granular breakdown of features) and mapped against the customer journey. The reason for mapping these stories across the user journey is to ensure that a collection of stories (the thin slice) can be released to a subset of customers for early feedback (see Figure 6-6). The reason to move away from just mapping features is that features can typically be broken down further (into user stories), which helps us prioritize a much thinner slice to test with.

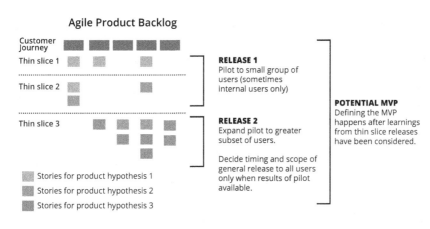

Figure 6-6

Thin slicing a product into multiple releases across the customer journey.

Thin slicing helps teams get started on the smallest learning opportunity while continuously testing hypotheses to get to a viable product. It is often about defining multiple releases prior to releasing the MVP (see Figure 6-6). Typically, multiple thin slices can be released for early feedback from a pilot set of customers, long before the MVP is available. This step is a useful way to encourage smaller, incremental delivery. A great deal can be learned by releasing smaller, thinner slices. In addition to the important customer feedback received, important internal organizational pieces will help set up the team for continuous learning. Some examples of organizational improvement and learning include the answers to these questions:

- Can we shorten the time it takes from feature definition to having it in customers' hands?
- What are the obstacles in our path to production?
- Can we set up the delivery infrastructure to release often?
- Can we access real customer data that is accessible from day 1?
- Do we have a stable environment for customer testing?
- Have we defined our pilot customers? What is the lead time for recruiting them? What communication and expectations need to be set?

Thin slicing is an activity that is typically done with a self-sufficient team at the beginning of product definition, but also takes place incrementally during product build and releases. Typically every 2 months is a good cadence. More experienced teams meet to review thin slices as needed, sometimes as frequently as every 2 weeks for 15 minutes. A thin slicing workshop has the following objectives:

- Obtain alignment of many opinions of what a first release (and subsequent releases) could be across a broad stakeholder group (e.g., product, distribution, marketing, finance)
- Identify hypotheses you want to validate that may cause a pivot in direction
- Minimize uncertainty around the product idea by releasing an end-to-end slice of the product as early as possible to a small subset of customers for feedback

Thin slicing starts with understanding the end-to-end customer journey, defining clear customer goals, mapping outcomes or features at each step in the journey, and then relatively prioritizing thin slices that can be released to the customer for validation and feedback. This creates the "build, measure, learn" loop in agile delivery. During the first few thin slices of your product, feedback should focus on validating problem–solution fit and defining the next thin slice of the product to build. When a substantial number of customers are providing usage feedback, quantitative data can start to drive the next slices using techniques such as A/B testing and customer analytics.

Example of Thin Slice Definitions

(Continuing the earlier healthcare distribution example)

We were working for a healthcare organization that was interested in replacing an existing product that enabled matching of thousands of lines of product codes to facilitate identification of the best product fit-to-price combination. We had a hypothesis that a machine (through fuzzy matching) could outperform what a human currently does manually.

The first thin slice delivered involved running the algorithm manually, with a basic front end that compared the results from the old way to the new way. If the algorithm was not successful (i.e., the hypothesis was proven wrong), our team would change direction and focus instead on improving identification of products that needed manual attention through improved visualizations. Some of the additional features that were not considered critical to learning, such as the ability to share the output, filtering, and sorting, were identified in slice 3. We learned during slice 1 that some of those filters and sorting of data were critical to achieving the desired user goal, so we prioritized our backlog to include some of the higher-value interactions earlier.

Product MVP Slice Definition

Initial product MVP hypothesis:

- We believe *automating the data matching of inventory used by hospitals*
- Will result in *greater savings in products purchased and consumed*
- Which we will validate *by comparing savings realized for 3 hospitals and 10 market baskets.*

If this hypothesis is proven true, the product will have achieved product–solution fit for 3 hospitals (unique customer segments and data needs), and we will continue to invest in the product for future hospitals.

First Thin Slice Definition

First thin slice hypothesis:

- We believe *improving the data matching of inventory used by hospitals*
- Will result in *lower-cost products without compromising quality*
- Which we will validate by *running semi-automated matching (without machine learning) with a subset of data and comparing cost savings of products that are considered "like for like" in quality and purpose.*

When it came to running the experiment, the team further refined the experiment to the following:

- We believe *matching 10,000 lines of product code for 1 pilot hospital with our custom algorithm*
- Will result in *time savings of 1–2 hours and improve matches* by 10–20%
- Which we will measure *by comparing time and accuracy of product matches using the old way versus the new way.*

Second Thin Slice Definition (Assumes Slice 1 Is Successful)

Operationalize the algorithm and incorporate it into the new product. Include improved data visualizations to support exception handling.

(At the time of defining slices, slice 2 and beyond were placeholders and therefore not worded in terms of hypotheses to validate. Later, the team came back to define what we wanted to validate in slices 2, 3, and so on. For this product, completion of slice 4 was considered the viable product.)

Third Thin Slice Definition

Improved user interactions through sorting, filtering, and data analysis.

Fourth Thin Slice Definition

Scale the product from 100 to 1000 users (placeholder until higher-priority hypotheses are proven).

Architectural Considerations

The first thin slice of a product enables delivery teams to bring forward technical unknowns, risks, and complexity that enable the proposed architecture to evolve while proving out technical assumptions and approaches. Driving a thin slice down through the architectural layers (see Figure 6-7) allows teams to prove out approaches to integration, testing, and data integrity. Teams are then able to validate core assumptions earlier, and thereby progress on a path that enables more rapid build and release. Chapter 2, Tech@Core, describes the process of creating a tech radar for incorporating technology trends and reducing technical debt as part of this evolution.

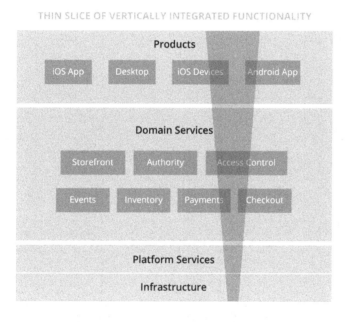

Figure 6-7
Taking a thin slice of vertically integrated functionality.

Final Thoughts

A product mindset is a capability that stresses delivering customer value in the present and adaptability for the future. Building a product mindset is often overlooked, but is an important capability in digital transformations. This mindset requires a fundamental shift in the way traditional stakeholders (portfolio teams) and delivery teams work together to create alignment on what's most important, and work together to incrementally validate hypotheses about customer needs, technical considerations, and business benefits expected to be realized.

An organization can have a clearly articulated strategy, but until the whole organization—including delivery teams—is able to deliver the assumed value (or recommend initiatives be killed because assumptions were incorrect), realization of investments will be limited.

Chapter 7

Integrating Strategic and Business as Usual Portfolios

Chapters 4, Building a Value-Driven Portfolio, and 5, Measuring and Prioritizing Value, introduced you to the Lean Value Tree (LVT) and Measures of Success (MoS), focusing primarily on strategic goals—namely, making your way toward a digital enterprise. If you are lucky, maybe 10 to 20 percent of your budget can be spent on strategic initiatives. The other 80 to 90 percent will go toward activities that are typically labeled Business as Usual (BAU). Even if you plan to spend, say, 15 percent of the budget on new initiatives, short-term demands and the raw magnitude of the BAU budget will often pull resources away from your new initiatives. This is another area where it takes courageous executives and leaders to overcome the inertia of BAU. This chapter addresses the critical components of work that need to be addressed: work from your strategic LVT, work to maintain or enhance current BAU systems, and work to enhance and develop capabilities.

Back to Reality

There are a number of questions you need to address in this reality check:

- Which workflow components need to be prioritized?
- How do we balance priorities for these seemingly disparate components?

- What kinds of MoS do we use for BAU items?
- What are the factors that make the approach outlined in this chapter effective?

Integrated Backlogs

One of the advantages of agile software development comes from the team's ability to focus on a few valuable things each iteration. Productivity suffers in any team, whether agile or not, when priorities are unclear or when items are injected into the work stream from unplanned sources. Frequent task switching and lack of an effective way to prioritize work both adversely impact effective work time.

Chapter 5 provided the basics of prioritizing strategic workflows. Of course, other workflows that impinge on delivery teams' time also need to be addressed.

Teams produce more value when they have a well-prioritized backlog of work to pull from as they are ready. But what do you do with all that interrupt-driven work that consumes the majority of any delivery team's time once their product has been released to customers? What about small enhancement ideas and defects that come from users after the release? This type of work has been known by many names—break/fix, maintenance, bug fixes, patches, and others. Typically, this work is pushed onto the delivery team because they are the obvious choice to change their own code. Certainly, this is a correct assumption, but the team wasn't planning for this work and taking it up jeopardizes their existing commitments to new strategic features. In the alternative case, these small but unscheduled changes may be handled by a maintenance team, which creates another set of problems.

This prioritization problem plagues every team attempting to deliver software. It gets worse when you consider the tech debt that accumulates during product development and maintenance. The cumulative effect slows the team down and makes development more challenging. Eventually, this reaches a nexus when the team is forced to deal with the sins of their past. Tech debt consumes their capacity and reduces, at least temporarily, the value they deliver to their customers. These customers are not happy that they are not getting many new features in the next release.

What about all those neat new ideas? Small changes that are valuable and don't take a lot of time to deliver, it seems as if it makes sense to just "slip those in" the next release. Of course, that also impacts the planned work schedule. All of these types of work are important and have to be addressed, but without the typical unpredictable impact on the planned work.

The title of this section deliberately includes the word "backlogs," rather the singular "backlog." The "s" is important. Each delivery team would have a backlog for its initiatives. Under a bet there might be two initiatives, each of which is assigned to a different team, so that each team would have its own backlog. At the next level up, each goal team would have a backlog of prioritized bets. However, the emphasis in this chapter will be on the initiative backlog used by delivery teams.

Backlog Components

Figure 7-1 shows the components of a backlog—Strategic, Defects, Technical Debt, Small Enhancements, and Technical Capability. Each of these components takes time and needs to be prioritized. Three will be considered part of BAU (inside the dotted-line box). This section describes each of these components and the next section goes into more detail about how to prioritize them.

Strategic

The bottom level of the LVT contains strategic initiatives that are broken down into stories that incorporate the product ideas described in Chapter 6, Building a Product Mindset. In our experience, for most organizations only 10 to 20 percent of the work is strategic. Most portfolios consist of mainly the other three types of work listed under BAU.

Figure 7-1
Components of
backlogs.

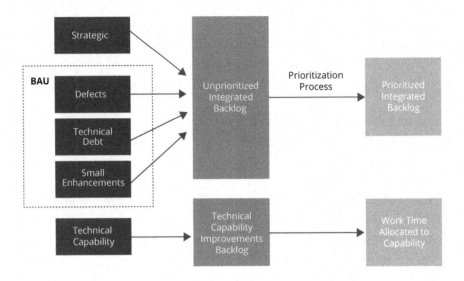

Business as Usual

Every organization has legacy systems. The older your organization, the larger
the investment in those legacy systems and they consume significant delivery
capacity. We refer to this non strategic work as BAU, and break it down into
three main types—small enhancements, defects, and technical debt.

First, an important governance question for BAU work is, "Do we use
an LVT?" The answer is, "It depends." There are advantages and disadvan-
tages to either approach. The advantage of putting BAU items on the LVT is
that your entire workload will be depicted in one place and you can see how
BAU work impacts strategic work. The disadvantage of putting BAU items
on the LVT is that when you try to map all of your BAU work, you will have
a significantly larger tree. Moreover, much of it cannot be directly mapped
to your business strategy, as that strategy usually does not specify maintaining your current capabilities.

Imagine how you might try to map the small enhancements to various
corporate reporting systems into an LVT. Some changes might be driven by
your desire to understand a part of your business better—to pursue a new
market segment, or to improve the efficiency of a business process. These
could be incorporated into the goals and bets that describe that strategy, but

many of them likely are not really clearly called out in your business strategy, and don't have a home in the LVT. In that case, you need to "invent" groupings of this work to represent them in the goal–bet–initiative structure of the LVT, thereby obscuring strategic clarity.

Depending on the nature of your organization and the portfolio size, you might accept these tradeoffs. If your company is like most of the large organizations we have worked with, the incorporation of BAU in the LVT actually defeats the purpose of the tool, so you need another way of handling it. Let's first describe the various types of BAU work, and then outline an approach to managing and prioritizing it.

Types of BAU Work

BAU can span a range of work types and time commitments. While a number of terms are used to categorize this work, the three used in this chapter are small enhancements, defects, and technical debt. These are shown in Figure 7-2, together with strategic work, to provide a total view of a team's workload.

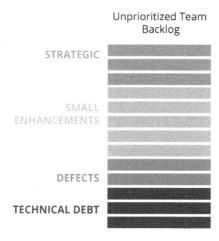

Figure 7-2
Unprioritized team backlog components.

Small Enhancements

Many organizations have "maintenance teams" that take care of legacy systems. These teams handle the small enhancement requests from various user representatives. Such small enhancements are typically driven by a desire to make things better, faster, or cheaper.

Often there are governance rules to keep these small changes within limits. Maximum investment limits, usually expressed as the number of person-hours estimated to complete the work, are the typical ones we see with our clients.

These maintenance items are seen as the "fast path" to get things done because they rarely require jumping through the cost/benefit analysis hurdles for large projects. Unfortunately, such requests are also often abused and lead to investment in work that was rejected by the investment committee (or would have been, if it had been scrutinized). On a positive note, small enhancements represent a way to bottle up all the investment leakage, and at least contain it within a budget that can be managed. Some organizations are quite good at using product leadership and user committees to prioritize this work and spend that money wisely. Others, not so much.

Defects

Complex problems tend to drive complex solutions that are not always implemented perfectly. In software, development mistakes (sometimes called "bugs" so they sound less ominous) are often made and need to be corrected. We have seen organizations with significant software quality problems that are spending 50 percent of their budgets on defect repairs. Even the best organization with less than 5 percent spending on defect repairs still needs a way to manage the work. Incident and problem management are beyond the scope of this book, but all organizations, regardless of the magnitude of their investment in defect repairs, should have effective and efficient incident and problem management processes.[1]

The most challenging part of defect repair work is that much of it is unplanned. While usually the work needed to effect the repair is minimal, that's not always the case. When incidents occur, service needs to be restored quickly. In most organizations, incidents with high impact are prioritized and override all other work until resolved. This really throws a wrench into prioritization and portfolio management.

1. For a good starting point on incident and problem management, see The Stationery Office, ed. *ITIL Practitioner Guidance.* Norwich, CT: The Stationery Office, 2016.

Technical Debt

As defined in Chapter 2, Tech@Core, technical debt is defined as the degradation of technology over time due to a lack of investment in maintaining adaptability and quality.[2] Technical debt causes cycle time to decrease from release to release, and even from iteration to iteration. It accumulates over time—slowly at first, but and then faster and faster as you abandon quality for "one-time" speed. As with financial debt, allowing technical debt to go unpaid means accumulating a significant penalty in the form of reduced adaptability and stability.

Best practice would encourage "managing" technical debt so that the penalty never becomes a material negative impact on the business. Therefore, you need to incorporate this type of work into your BAU portfolio management process along with the other types of BAU work.

MoS for BAU

Good measures of success are critical for all teams to have the necessary information to understand what is expected and to be able to evaluate its impact. For the strategic work, described in Chapters 4 and 5, the LVT can help structure the strategic portfolio, and MoS articulate the desired outcome. But how do you do this for the rest of the work—that is, BAU?

One of the best places to look for guidance on structuring the rest of the work is the fundamental business capabilities of the organization. All organizations have a core set of business capabilities that constitute their value generation capability. BAU work is typically a combination of repairing defects, managing technical debt, and making small enhancements to the systems that support those capabilities. These processes are relatively stable, and business outcome-oriented measurements usually already exist or can be identified for them.

2. Ward Cunningham has a short video explaining his thinking around coining the term "technical debt": Cunningham, Ward. *Debt Metaphor*. https://www.youtube.com/watch?v=pqeJFYwnkjE. Accessed January 21, 2019.

Capabilities

This book has focused on narrowing a wide range of opportunities to your specific goals using the LVT. However, there are two related types of capability development—business and technical. An example of a business capability would be an order fulfillment process, whereas a technical capability would be building a technology platform. BAU business capabilities are improved by intermittent small enhancements, whereas technical capabilities are enhanced by activities such as skills training. So you might have a strategic opportunity goal that is partially supported by enhancing a business capability, which in turn is supported by a new technical capability. An enhancement to a business capability would generate a delivery story to be prioritized, while a technical capability would be incorporated by assigning a percentage of the team's effort to an improvement activity.

Business Capability-Based Portfolios

Each business capability has one or more business processes and associated systems that support them. The stakeholders responsible for these business capabilities typically have a set of key performance indicators (KPIs) or process measurements that they use to manage the performance and health of the capabilities in their charge. For example, every organization has finance and accounting capabilities that are necessary for it to function as a business. Most would agree that these capabilities are not strategic, but certainly critical to the functioning of the business. Using accounts receivable (AR) as an example, we typically find measurements like "days sales outstanding" (DSO) as a performance metric. There is a clear understanding by people who work in the AR department that they need to manage DSO to a minimum number.

Imagine in a large organization that there was enough BAU work to establish an AR portfolio. You have a clear set of stakeholders who are responsible for AR. You have a set of systems that support AR and that delineate the responsibility for the technology assets. Typically, a budget is associated with this capability to pay for the people, systems, and other operational costs, so you have an investment pool to manage. These are all the criteria needed to manage a portfolio of BAU work using the same concepts, tools, and techniques described for the strategic portfolios from the LVT.

A BAU portfolio is a backlog of the three types of work—small enhancements, defects, and technical debt—that need to be managed within a budget. Our principle of maximizing value can be applied to prioritizing the work and to demonstrating the value created.

The responsible AR stakeholders typically have a set of KPIs with targets like our DSO example. They are constantly looking for ways to improve DSO by making changes to the business processes, which almost always drive changes to the supporting systems. Thus, you have a steady flow of small enhancement requests into the backlog. Defects are discovered and fixed. Technical debt is accumulated when the team trades short-term expediency for long-term stability.

All this AR-related work has a direct impact on DSO. If you stop investing in small enhancements, little or no progress on minimizing DSO would be made. If the organization was satisfied with the current DSO, or believed a higher value could be obtained elsewhere, then money (which is correlated with capacity) could be redirected to another portfolio, such as accounts payable. This ability to understand the value of every portfolio is at the heart of EDGE. Whether it is applied to moving investment funds from one strategic initiative to another under a bet, or moving those funds from one BAU portfolio to another, the same lightweight governance processes[3] can be applied.

Technical Capability

The LVT and MoS help us understand which opportunities to pursue to compete in the marketplace. Capability or continuous improvement activities are the work in which the team invests to improve their value-generating capacity. By developing an integrated backlog, you are trying to understand the entire workload of your delivery teams and gain a more comprehensive understanding of the product performance and investment. Continuously improving your engineering capabilities takes time. Allocating time to work on strategic initiatives is hard enough; allocating time to work on improving your engineering capability is even harder. Nevertheless, you need to make this continuous improvement work visible and prioritize it along with the rest of your work.

3. See the periodic value review in Chapter 8, Lightweight Governance.

Improving technical capabilities is different from delivering customer stories. As such, and referring back to Figure 7-1, the time needed to improve capabilities should be allocated by percentage to teams. This percentage may vary from time to time as the mix of strategic and BAU work changes. We strongly recommend that you take a slow and steady approach to continually improving your engineering capability. Technology and engineering techniques continually evolve, and your capability needs to evolve as well.

Two Percent for Continuous Improvement

Years ago, when working as a CIO, David was able to convince the CFO of his organization that the IT department should invest at least 2 percent of the total IT budget every year into continuous improvement activities. These activities consisted of a mix of tools, learning, and development, and even some technology spikes that were not requested by the business, but were undertaken for the purpose of learning and demonstrating proof of concepts for new engineering techniques.

One memorable example was a $185,000 investment in improving automated environment deployment, which unlocked an average of 21 percent improvement in team velocity for seven delivery teams. That 21 percent more work was like hiring another team at no cost. Of course, that totally understates the value created by applying that capacity to high-value work. That investment had the highest ROI of any investment made by the company that year.

Combining Strategic and BAU Portfolios

As mentioned earlier, most organizations spend more than 80 percent of their capacity on BAU work. Many portfolios of work will never include any strategic work at all. Our accounts receivable portfolio is a good example: Rarely will a strategic initiative change the fundamental business capability of AR. For the sake of clarity, let's imagine your innovative colleagues came up with a strategic initiative that required changes to AR. You generally want to keep strategic initiatives separate from BAU items, but occasionally smaller strategic items can be managed in the BAU portfolio. When this happens, how do you manage this work? In which portfolio does it belong?

One approach to combining strategic and BAU portfolios that works well is the concept of reserved capacity. In our AR BAU portfolio example, if some strategic work is likely, you could reserve some of the money (capacity) invested in the AR budget for strategic work, as depicted in Figure 7-3. This approach maintains a consistent budget for operational expenses, but allows for a small amount of potential strategic work. These funds can be used only for small strategic initiatives in the AR BAU portfolio. The reserve capacity should be taken into account when establishing targets for the MoS of the AR BAU portfolio. If no strategic work is required, the team is expected to use that capacity to generate value through BAU. Larger strategic initiatives should be handled in an LVT portfolio and prioritized using the process defined in Chapter 5.

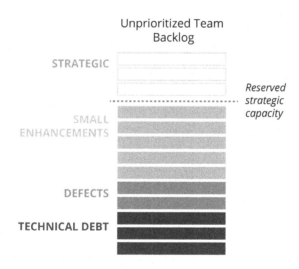

Figure 7-3
Reserved capacity for strategic work in BAU portfolios.

Prioritization

Recall that Figure 7-1 contains an unprioritized list of items that the delivery teams needs to prioritize for their next iteration. If there is an existing prioritized backlog, as there will be in most cases, you will be adjusting the list by adding new items and removing obsolete ones.

Traditional Solutions

In the past, many IT organizations divided work into new projects and maintenance. Defects, new feature additions, infrastructure updates, and other small changes were handled by the maintenance group. Individuals often worked on these small changes by themselves. Further, the more experienced and skilled people wanted to work on projects and not "cleanup" work, which left less experienced staff destined to work on maintenance. Maintenance work was usually high priority, so quick fixes that increased technical debt often became the norm. Because new-project teams didn't have to worry about the long-term consequences of their work, and because the project schedule and costs usually drove that work, quality (including testing) often suffered.

Many teams we have worked with have tried various techniques to deal with these challenges. Setting aside a portion of the team's capacity for this type of work is one common approach. This approach definitely helps eliminate the negative impact on the planned work schedule—or does it? We would argue that all you have done is to guarantee that you deliver less planned work every iteration.

Here is an example. You might understand from your performance data that, on average, you have 8 story points of defect repairs every iteration. You reason that if your team burns at 30 story points[4] per iteration, you can commit to delivering only 22 points of planned work in each subsequent iteration. You would be correct if you really had 8 points of defect repairs in the next iteration. But what happens if a really bad bug is uncovered and 16 points are needed to handle it? You want to squash that nasty bug, but you don't have the budget to do so without giving up some planned work. You are back in the same prioritization quandary. Now think about the opposite scenario—when you don't have any defects to deal with. You have excess capacity and could accept another story, but this may set the wrong expectation about your ongoing value-generating capacity.

---

4. Story points are an activity measure, not a performance (MoS) measure.

One reason that organizations often separate their planned and unplanned work backlogs is because they have no method of comparing the various types of work for prioritization. We are often asked, "How do I compare a new feature request with a bug?" You use an understanding of customer and business value to guide you.

A Better Way

Transparency and giving teams substantial decision-making authority are better ways of managing this problem. Having a visible backlog that includes all types of work (strategic, BAU, and technical capabilities) gives the team, product specialist, and customers situational awareness. This is a good foundation for a collaborative effort to prioritize work. A stakeholder with a new idea can see what else is on the team's plate when bringing up that new idea. In our experience, this often influences the quality of the ideas that are added to the backlog. One way this happens is through demand shaping, in which stakeholders with new ideas look at the existing backlog before they add to it. They might decide that their requirement is already satisfied by an existing story. Regardless, when the inevitable discussion of "when can I have it…" comes around, the stakeholder and the product specialists are likely to be more understanding of each other's position. Working this way reduces uncomfortable conversations, and instead makes them more collaborative and productive.

Because you have organized your portfolios by outcomes and have good measures of success, you can apply relative value prioritization techniques similar to those described in Chapter 5. By scoring the relative impact using MoS and the relative effort, all types of work can be compared. In addition, each category (e.g., strategic, BAU) needs decision-making guidance. While the LVT goals are articulated, you may need to work on this guidance for other types of work.

> **High Value for Defect Repair**
>
> Sometimes evaluating the relative values of enhancements and bug fixes is not difficult. Many years ago, the Social Security Administration discovered that checks being delivered to recipients were incorrect. A recent software update contained a calculation error. Each individual difference was small, but the magnitude of the error became large when those small problems were multiplied by millions of recipients. It would not be difficult to determine that this "bug" fix had the highest priority.

A point about defect repair work: Some teams have struggled with how to apply this approach. They say something like, "This is a bug; it doesn't add any value." We would argue that if it is a bug, then it must be preventing some value from being realized. If that is indeed the case, then fixing the bug should unlock that value. If it truly doesn't make any difference to your MoS, then that work will end up at the bottom of your priority list, and rightly so.

Technical debt is another type of work that has historically been difficult to prioritize. Thinking about tech debt in terms of the value that it prevents you from realizing helps puts this cost in perspective. If your product goal is to deliver a continuous stream of value, then technical debt reduction becomes important because doing so enhances both speed and adaptability over time.

There is no magic formula for making prioritization decisions. Balancing between working on initiatives, products, BAU, staff capabilities, and technical debt depends on reasonable value analysis and a collaborative decision-making frame of mind. This process can be enhanced by certain practices, effective judgment, and escalation procedures. Moreover, while you try to push as many decisions to the autonomous delivery teams as possible, you can't push them all. Sometimes managers and executives have perspectives that team members don't. Sometimes major spending decisions are necessary. Pulling all these components into an integrated, prioritized backlog is challenging, but ultimately worth the effort.

Component Strategies

The team needs guidance for each component of its portfolio. For strategic stories, you can obtain the most comprehensive strategy information from the goals, bets, initiatives, and MoS. For technical debt, you can use the asset or asset class strategies discussed in Chapter 2, Tech@Core. For defect repair, you have business capability-based MoS. And, finally, you have the articulated product strategy described in Chapter 6. Teams that have, and understand, these goals have a solid basis on which to make prioritization decisions. Those that don't are doomed to flounder around trying to prioritize components without guidance.

Let's consider an example of how this guidance can impact decision making. If your executive team stresses that strategic components have a very high current priority, they might also add that enhancements should be very limited for a time. At the same time, you might emphasize technical debt reduction so as to improve delivery speed and adaptability while the new product is being built.

You have bet and initiative strategies that provide detail-level guidance. For example, by knowing and understanding a bet-level hypothesis, the team has an incentive to give higher priority to stories that will quickly prove or disprove that hypothesis.

Relative versus Absolute Value

We have emphasized, particularly in Chapter 5, our preference for a relative (rather than absolute) prioritization process. A relative process is much faster than spending time calculating concrete numbers that are often based on suspicious assumptions. Relative prioritization also enhances your ability to include intangible factors in your deliberations. No matter what techniques you use, the final prioritized backlog—at any level—boils down to a collective judgment.

The final factor that favors relative prioritization is the quick feedback that brings you back on track if your team's judgment takes a brief leave of absence. When your feedback loop is many months in duration, the tendency is to spend far too much time analyzing to get everything right the first time. Your real goal should be to get everything right the *last* time.

Doing Less

We have encountered organizations in which the Portfolio Management Office processes many, many requests for projects, and its denizens dutifully go about defining the requests, calculating ROI, and adding them to a large backlog. Sometimes the low-priority items stay on the backlog for years. The hours spent calculating costs, prioritizing, and reprioritizing these items can be staggering, representing a large sunk cost. We've seen backlogs with 1000 projects, of which maybe 100 have a chance of ever being funded. How do you avoid all this wasted effort in EDGE? Demand shaping, delaying detail, and quick quartiling.

If requesters can throw new work into the hopper on a whim, without consequence, then the backlog will inevitably grow. In contrast, if the product team has a good understanding of the items on each workflow and on the backlog, they will be less likely to add to that backlog. Keeping undesirable items off the backlog in the first place by evaluating all items—whether for LVT plan or technical debt—keeps the teams from wasting effort.

Agile Development Also Shapes Demand

Several years ago, Jim worked with a Canadian medical instrument company that was developing a new application for its sales and marketing department. "We have these 100 very important features we want in this application," the marketing owner said. "Fine," replied the development manager. "What are the top three priority items you need?" "Oh, no," voiced the owner. "We have to have all 100." "Granted," said the director, "but let us deliver the top 3 in a few iterations and then we will tackle what comes next." After delivering those 3 items, the next question was, of course, "What are the next 3?" Again, the owner said, "But we need all the rest of the 97 features." "Oh, don't worry, we will give you all 97, but let's resume by delivering the next 3 on your priority list." This went on several more times until approximately 20 features had been delivered and deployed to the customer. When the director went back to the owner and asked,

"So what are your next 3?", the owner responded, "Well, the first 20 are really delivering most of the value we needed. We don't see the need right now for the last 80. We will get back to you later if we need them."

As the director related this story to a conference audience, he said, "If we had used our traditional process of developing requirements for all 100 items and then implementing them, we would have done all 100 and might as well have piled money on the table and lit it on fire."

Agile practices help identify *what not to do* as well as *what to do*. This demand shaping is one of the more powerful aspects of agile development that often goes unappreciated.

Delaying detail is another way to reduce work effort, if not demand itself. In the example with a backlog of 1000 items, suppose demand shaping reduced this backlog to 600 items. Should you then develop story-level details for all 600? No. If your velocity was 10 stories per iteration developing details for all 600 would be wasted effort. Detailing enough for two or three iterations of delivery should, in most cases, be sufficient.

Quick quartiling is another way to do less. Rather than prioritizing all the items on your backlog, try breaking that list into quarters or even thirds first—labeled, for example, "must," "high," "moderate," and "low" priority. Again, it's a way to move through the prioritization process faster. Don't do work you don't need to—do less!

Team Prioritization

A key reason that the prioritization approach advanced in this chapter works is that it is conducted by a collaborative, self-sufficient, autonomous team. If the organization lacks a high degree of collaborative decision making, teams are not self-sufficient with broad knowledge, and teams lack the autonomy to make most prioritization decisions, then the practices in this chapter won't work well. The Agile Manifesto states, "Individuals and teams over process and tools." The skills, abilities, and experience of team members are the source of good judgment. Using this same prioritization process without the essential elements of a self-sufficient,[5] autonomous team will lead to problematic results.

Team judgment is needed because items in your workflow may have different MoS. If an item from the LVT plan has an MoS of customer clicks whereas an item from the BAU list uses DSO, that inconsistency makes prioritization tricky. In the case of items with different MoS flowing into the process, relative ranking of value using the collective knowledge of the team works much better.

There is also an impact on prioritization when you organize by product rather than by project orientation. Traditional project-organized teams emphasized speedy feature delivery without giving much attention to the other components, particularly if maintenance was then handed off to another team. They had little incentive to "balance" components. In a product-centered team, the product specialists are as responsible for balancing priorities among components as the tech staff are. They have to live with the long-term consequences of their decisions, as does the tech staff.

Work-in-Progress

The ideas of monitoring and restricting work-in-progress (WIP) have had a large influence in the agile, lean, and Kanban communities. It is a waste of time to prioritize 300 items on a team's backlog when the team delivers only 10 items per iteration. The introduction of new items or changing priorities will alter the sequence in your backlog over time. As shown in Figure 7-4, restricting the number of items flowing from the unprioritized to the prioritized boxes will save time. The size of the two boxes reflects this reality. Limiting WIP appears to be easy—but it's not. It takes a lot of discipline to limit workflow to the capacity of the team. It means saying "Not yet" to customers.

---

5. Self-sufficient autonomous teams have members from product, IT, IT operations, and other knowledge areas.

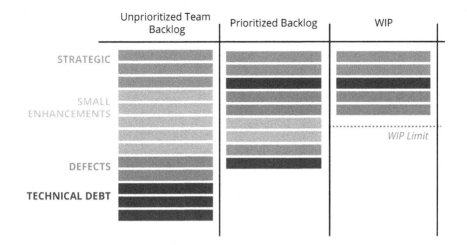

Unprioritized Team Backlog	Prioritized Backlog	WIP
STRATEGIC		
SMALL ENHANCEMENTS		
		WIP Limit
DEFECTS		
TECHNICAL DEBT		

Figure 7-4
Managing your backlog.

> **Note**
>
> Several years ago, Jim was talking with the director of a large state agency who was concerned about his IT group's slow delivery, lack of urgency, and low overall production. "How many people do you have on staff?" was the first question. "Forty-two," replied the director. "And how many active projects is the staff working on now?" was the second question. "Forty-three," replied the director, suddenly realizing what his answer implied.

Value and Effort Scoring

This section brings together all of the prioritization factors just described. This value and effort scoring is the last step in assigning priorities to the various components. The section in Chapter 5 on value and effort scoring provided the basis for setting priorities for the different types of work. A story is an increment of work that delivers value to the customer at the end of an iteration. While a technical debt item may be different from a small enhancement item, we will still utilize stories to describe these smallest units of work. This is the lowest level at which teams will establish priorities. Following are four practices you can use for prioritizing stories, presented from the simplest to the most complex. All of these practices involve the whole delivery team in the process. Value scoring again gives us a way to compare very different components and prioritize them.

Simplest: Direct Priority Assignment

The simplest and least time-consuming prioritization process is to have the team infer value by just ranking the stories on the backlog. Although the team members understand all of the factors involved—such as strategies, cost, value, and risk—they just don't take the time to assign specific numerical weights to them.

Moderately Simple: Direct Value Assignment

The next step in simple to complex ways of assessing priority is to assign a numeric value to a story and possibly an effort number. As mentioned in Chapter 5, you might use a gross measurement scale such as "Low, Medium, High," or T-shirt sizes (S, M, L), or Fibonacci numbers (1, 2, 3, 5, 8, …). Because stories are often similar in size (they do not have the size range of bets, for example), you may not want to estimate an effort number. Figure 7-5 shows an assignment matrix using both value and effort. In this approach, the priority is not calculated, but rather assigned by the team as it looks over the matrix. You would not bother to take the time to calculate the value/effort (V/E) ratio if effort was not used.

Figure 7-5
Prioritizing stories.

STORY	VALUE	EFFORT	PRIORITY
Story 1	1	1	4
Story 2	2	3	3
Story 3	5	1	1
Story 4	1	5	5
Story 5	3	3	2

Moderate: MoS Assessment

In Figure 5-4, three different MoS (NPS, conversion, abandonment) were evaluated to come up with the value score. Then in Figure 5-5, three different effort categories were assessed (investment, risk, change) to determine the effort score. After each of these value and effort numbers were assigned, the rest was a calculation, as was the V/E number that combined value and effort. In the two simpler approaches, the effort numbers were implied rather than explicit. At the level of stories in the backlog, it may not be worth the extra effort of using this MoS assessment approach. That said, the team may want to conduct a more complex analysis in the beginning when they are still learning about the process and each other. Once they feel comfortable that the extra effort isn't necessary, they can select one of the simpler approaches.

Complex: Cost of Delay

Chapter 5 introduced the idea of using Cost of Delay (CoD) to determine value. While you might potentially use CoD at the story level, we think it far too complex and time consuming to use it for prioritizing LVT components within most organizations.

Escalation Processes

Although you want teams and product owners to understand the total scope of work that the team has on its backlog to make prioritization decisions, there will be times when external factors or management needs dictate that organization leaders need to engage in priority setting. Having an escalation process in place will help the teams understand which prioritization decisions they can make and which ones need leadership input.

Sometimes teams will have difficulty sorting through the relative priorities among the four components. While you try to have value measures for each item, it is sometimes difficult to decide, for example, whether a BAU enhancement or a technical debt story has more relative value. No matter how jelled a team, there will inevitably be situations in which differences of opinion between team members can't be reconciled. For example, a product person may feel the pressure of new features, whereas the technical staff may think a technical debt reduction should have higher priority.

This may be the point at which a well-functioning autonomous team and a team that's not quite there take different approaches. The latter team may think they are at an impasse, so they escalate the decision to management. Given that the well-functioning team has the appropriate mix of product and technical members, they should be able to handle a very high percentage of difficult prioritization decisions. Of course, there will always be situations where decisions will need to be escalated to higher management levels.

Imperfect Prioritization

When prioritizing backlog items, it is all too easy to think that a particular set of priorities is fixed. But this is an adaptive process that uses relative, not absolute, measures, so priorities will likely change from time to time.

> **Too Flexible?**
>
> Years ago a client was complaining about a team's zero velocity (no stories completed) for several iterations. The inexperienced product owner was changing priorities *during* the two-week iterations, so nothing was ever completed. We recommended no changes during an iteration, except in extenuating circumstances. Velocity improved (from zero) and the team learned that managing change didn't always mean changing something. They also learned that being too focused on iterations sometimes clouded their view of their overall goals.

Of course, no process is perfect when people are involved. You may argue that the process proposed here isn't perfect—and we would be the first to agree. But remember the story of two hikers in the woods upon encountering a grizzly bear. One hiker sat down and quickly put his running shoes on. "You can't outrun a bear in those shoes," said his companion. "I don't have to outrun the bear," the first hiker said, "I just have to outrun you." Our approach to prioritization doesn't have to be perfect; it just has to be better than your competitors' processes.

Remember that all the processes in EDGE are agile, meaning that there are short iterations of doing, followed by reflection and learning, and then by adapting quickly. Even if you get the priorities wrong, you get to adjust them in a short time period. Quick reaction to resolve mistakes provides a safety net for those mistakes and manages risk.

Final Thoughts

One important thing to keep in mind as you digest the practices in this chapter, as well as with practices in other chapters, is that you can't cherry pick those you think will benefit your organization and abandon others. Many of these practices fit together with each other, so you have to understand how they work in concert. In the early days of agile development when extreme programming began to gain popularity, some pundits complained that none of the practices were new. They were correct to some extent, but they missed the most important point: It was the *combination* of 12 practices and the value statements that were the big innovation. These practices worked in concert as an integrated whole. Take one away, and the whole weakened.

That's not to say that you can't adjust practices to suit your particular environment—early in this book, we noted that customization and adaptation is an important part of EDGE. However, you also need to understand how these practices support one another as you adapt them.

Chapter 8

Lightweight Governance

The agile value "working software over comprehensive documentation"[1] charged organizations to focus on the primary objective of software delivery—the code. Why was this so important? Because in many organizations the evolution of software engineering methods had taken a turn toward documents: lengthy requirements specifications, comprehensive test plans, extensive design diagramming, and more. These documents evolved over time to become the objective and code became a necessary, but less consequential, component. Agile isn't anti-documentation; instead, it favors the primary outcome of software development—running, tested code.

The Lost Objectives of Governance

You can apply the same analysis to governance. The real objectives of governance are to ensure that:

- Goals, bets, and initiatives meet their customer value goals.
- Decision-making rights required for accountability are effectively allocated and managed.

---

1. "Manifesto for Agile Software Development." Accessed February 28, 2019. https://agilemanifesto.org/.

- Initiatives are in compliance with internal and external regulations and standards (e.g., safety, auditing, accounting).

As with software delivery, the objectives of governance have gotten lost in the blizzard of documentation.[2] Jim once spoke at a conference put on by a major software engineering organization (he was on a panel debating the viability of this heavyweight approach). An indication of the extent to which documentation permeated the thinking was the conference feedback form—more than 20 pages in length.

A company that developed clinical trial medical software interpreted the Food and Drug Administration (FDA) requirement to map requirements to code to mean it had to complete the requirement specifications, then map them to code—eliminating the possibility of using iterative development. The company had to be convinced that it could do iterative development and then finish the mapping at the end. Similarly, many companies have misinterpreted Financial Accounting Standards Board (FASB)[3] for capitalizing costs and erroneously restricted agile development in that area.

The intention of lightweight governance is not to eliminate documentation, but rather to focus on the primary objectives of governance through appropriate delegation of decision rights and establishing clear accountability. Executives have a fiduciary responsibility to monitor investments. This oversight task is an important one—it keeps their organizations from making critical mistakes.

Establishing Lightweight Governance

Traditional portfolio and project governance stressed documenting deliverables (such as design and requirements documents) and completing activities. When using this approach, preparing for deliverable reviews with executives could be both exhaustive and scary. This phase-gate approach to

2. This chapter concentrates on portfolio governance, rather than overall technology governance.
3. FASB: Financial Accounting Standards Board. These standards have to do with categorization of costs to expense versus capital accounts.

managing risk delays progress and damages morale, as the process focuses on fiduciary control and a prescriptive plan. Adoption of agile delivery practices has worked against creating this type of environment, but unfortunately it has crept back in, as enterprises have tried to expand agile's reach to larger projects and across their organizations.

This emphasis on portfolio control is similar to traditional project management's focus on schedule and cost. With this approach, constraints, rather than value to the customer, become the focus. In EDGE, the focus is outcome oriented—geared toward customer value, innovation, and adaptation. Financial control, while important, is not the primary focus. The executive team's focus should be how to help the organization be faster, more innovative, and more adaptive—rather than slowing the process down. Every level of the executive teams should encourage speed and learning—which is exactly the intent of the "Establish lightweight governance" guideline.

EDGE governance is characterized by two key things: value monitoring, rather than activity monitoring; and speed and flexibility, rather than heavy process and documentation. Governance in your organization should be about steering value creation first. While governance certainly has a strong fiduciary aspect, management and executive reviewers provide unique perspectives and experience that can assist in effective delivery. Improved results come from collaboration and contribution, rather than strict control.

Portfolio Management at a Large Retailer

The CTO of a large retail company was frustrated. The development and operations groups had implemented agile and continuous delivery practices over the past few years, thereby improving delivery speed and putting the focus on more valuable projects. While its existing process worked—somewhat—in the past, it stymied the company's digital transformation efforts. The CTO was frustrated with its traditional portfolio management and processes.

The process to add projects to the portfolio, prioritize them, and release them to development was lengthy, and documentation was heavy and laborious. The retailer spent untold hours estimating costs for projects that were no more than a gleam in someone's eye—and then ended up so far down in the priority list that the analysis time was a complete waste. Furthermore, the Project Management Office (PMO) analysts spent far too many hours developing detailed benefit and return on investment (ROI) calculations that were never verified after the projects were implemented. All this effort, and making dozens of slides for presenting the results to management, meant that the process took months. Moreover, once the portfolio for the next year was decided upon, changes were seldom considered. In addition, the PMO staff and the CTO's development teams were constantly at odds.

In this organization, a lightweight, agile, fast delivery process was linked to the company strategy and goals by a slow, burdensome, heavyweight portfolio management process. The CTO's frustration was understandable. Our first step was to implement EDGE for the company's high-priority digital enterprise projects. This enabled a small change management effort to prove value with this different portfolio management approach.

Using the Lean Value Tree (LVT), we created outcome-oriented measures of success to prioritize work based on relative value within the portfolio. We also implemented frequent periodic value review cycles, which provided the ability to rebalance the portfolio more often than had been possible in the past.

The organization was able to quickly realize value with this approach. Leaders were able to align to the highest-priority goals and focus teams on what was most important. The CTO's frustration evolved into excitement. The culture evolved to an experimental mindset, with a constant reminder to work on the highest-value initiatives. That created a link between strategy and delivery that hadn't happened in the past. Subsequently, the use of EDGE increased for more of the retailer's overall portfolio.

Existing management frameworks, including governance, are the biggest roadblocks to business agility and product mindset. Many existing frameworks are documentation and process heavy, as people try to convince themselves they can predict the future by conducting extensive analysis. Many heavyweight practices arose, in part, because of mistakes—and the attempt to eliminate future mistakes. Unfortunately, those mistakes were often caused by events that couldn't be predicted when the plans were made. And you can't eliminate mistakes—no matter how many upfront documents or processes you implement. What you can do is to increase your ability to recognize mistakes earlier and respond rapidly, thereby mitigating losses and reducing risks.

Transformational initiatives—those requiring innovation—depend on learning faster, so small mistakes don't evolve into big ones. Approaching management frameworks like portfolio and program management from this new perspective demands leaders who are comfortable with being uncomfortable. It's not a place for the faint of heart.

Governance in EDGE stresses a regular cadence of Periodic Value Reviews (PVR). PVRs provide the framework to ensure that funds and resources are being used as intended and that progress toward goals, bets, and initiatives is being made. Your Value Realization Team (VRT) facilitates these reviews and ensures they are happening at an effective cadence. For an example of PVR cadence and participants, see Figure 8-1.

The three levels of review correspond to the LVT: goals, bets, and initiatives. The reviews give you a chance to determine if your current investments are still the right ones and to make decisions about changing investment strategies. At each level, reviewers decide whether investments should be stopped, pivoted, or expanded, or new investments should be made. Information they review includes progress on value created (Measures of Success [MoS]) for goals and bets, progress on delivery for initiatives, and investments made in each portfolio.

Figure 8-1

Periodic Value Review
cadence and lightweight
governance structure.

Goal Value Review

What: Ensure alignment of Goals to Strategic Vision and Investment Priorities and demonstrate customer value.

Frequency: Quarterly

Who: Executive Team and Goal Team

Bet Value Review

What: Ensure alignment of Bets to Goal and demonstrate customer value in bets.

Frequency: Monthly

Who: Goal Team and Bet Team

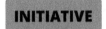

Initiative Review

What: Review progress on initiatives (part of iteration review, not separate meeting)

Frequency: Biweekly or in sync with delivery schedule

Who: Bet Team and Initiative Team

PVRs should have similar objectives to those of an agile delivery team's review:

- To encourage learning and early risk mitigation through short feedback cycles
- To make decisions based on value delivered first
- To decide, for each investment, whether to continue, adjust, stop, or pivot

The cadence of PVRs might be quarterly for goals, monthly for bets, and biweekly or weekly for initiatives. However, determining the cadence for your organization should begin by discussing the question, "How do we adapt fast enough?" It's not enough to have frequent reviews—your organization must be willing to make difficult allocation or reallocation decisions during these reviews. As we know too well, it's hard to kill initiatives (or bets or goals). It's hard to make decisions to reallocate funding from one bet to another. These decisions take courage, insight, and judgment (bolstered by

MoS data). Putting a "lightweight" process in place doesn't make hard decisions easier; in fact, it may make them harder because they have to be made quickly. The importance of lightweight governance is that it helps build organizational discipline through regular value reviews, and gives teams a forum in which to suggest new paths forward and assess the relative value of goals, bets, and initiatives.

Periodic Value Review

The PVR process shown in Figure 8-2 ensures an organization has an easy way to monitor and steer investments. The owner teams review value by evaluating the MoS.

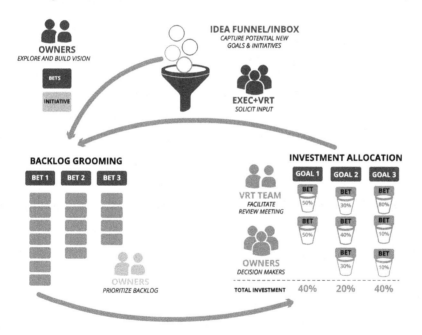

Figure 8-2
Periodic Value Review is a process for monitoring and steering investments.

In traditional portfolio management processes, rollups of portfolio status reports are used to communicate progress and surface problems that might be affecting the portfolio. These review processes tend to be focused on measures of activity (e.g., milestones achieved, budget spent), rather than on customer value achieved (e.g., customers can now view the status of their orders at payment).

EDGE replaces activity reviews with a PVR. At each level of the LVT, the owner teams review the value they've created during the period by showing the impact on the MoS. Because they've been delivering incrementally, they can demonstrate actual value creation (or lack thereof). This real-time feedback is a key differentiator of EDGE.

In traditional portfolio management, an organization has only visibility into the activity performed and knowledge of the original solution plan. It has very little opportunity to determine if it's prudent to continue on the original path, change direction, or stop the madness, because the result isn't known until the end. This is the fundamental failure of traditional portfolio management approaches: The organization has no ability to steer until it's too late. Its focus is on achieving the plan, whether or not that plan is still viable.

With a PVR, the owner teams consider the deliveries made, the value produced (MoS), the investments made, the work in progress, and the top of the backlog. This is a complete picture of the portfolio intended to provide enough information to support a value-based conversation between the stakeholders and the delivery team. The tone is collaborative and focused on continuing to foster the organization's strategy and vision.

Rebalancing the Portfolio

Rebalancing the portfolio occurs when information presented in the PVR indicates a change in the current investment. As an example, suppose a competitor releases a new product that requires an immediate response. That response might be to set up a new bet and take funds and teams from another opportunity to address it.

Specific questions to think about during the reviews include the following:

- Are we delivering the value anticipated for our MoS?
- Are we within our established constraint boundaries?
- Are investments in line with expectations?
- Are there any red flags?
- Are there any roadblocks that this review team can assist with?
- Are there any new external factors that we should be aware of?
- Are teams coming free soon for any other reason?
- Have we gained enough value that we should move on to the next backlog item in the portfolio?

The last question is particularly important—when should investment stop? you always have two choices, as shown in Figure 8-3: (1) continue and invest more or (2) stop and free up capacity to explore the next most valuable idea. Each review team should ask the question, "Do you want 100 percent of the value for 100 percent of the cost, or 90 percent of the value for 70 percent of the cost?" Often the last 10 to 30 percent of the cost provides minimal additional value. If enough value has been achieved, stop work on that item and move on to something new.

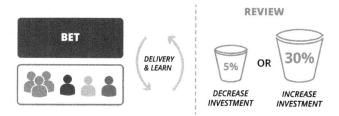

Figure 8-3

Adjusting investments based on Periodic Value Review.

Example: Using outcomes to steer investments. Investment may be increased if outcome is positive or decreased (stopped) if outcome is negative.

Value from a Cancelled Project

Our colleague Ken Collier tells a story about a project he worked on. His firm had delivered approximately 20 percent of the features to the client when the company cut back its investment portfolio and the project was suddenly without funds. When Ken and the client's IT staff presented the bad news, they added, "We could take another week or two and wrap up the project and fully deploy the 20 percent we have finished." "Great," said the client. "We are bummed the project was put on hold, but the features you have delivered so far have proved to be very valuable. Please go ahead and finish them."

If opportunities aren't delivering value, the organization can choose one of three options:

1. Invest less.
2. Stop pursuing an opportunity.
3. Pivot to a more valuable opportunity.

Investing less means setting new investment targets, adjusting staffing, and possibly adjusting MoS again. Stopping pursuit of an opportunity frees resources to take up the next most valuable opportunity. Pivoting means to use what you have learned to and continue a different way.

This regular and frequent response to feedback, shown in Figure 8-4, gives organizations unprecedented control over achieving business outcomes. Rebalancing—like all of EDGE—is incremental and iterative. Organizations needn't wait years to change direction. PVR teams have the opportunity with every PVR to react to their learning—to invest more in ideas that help, and to eliminate investment in ideas that don't.

Figure 8-4
Taking the next most valuable initiative from the backlog based on a PVR decision.

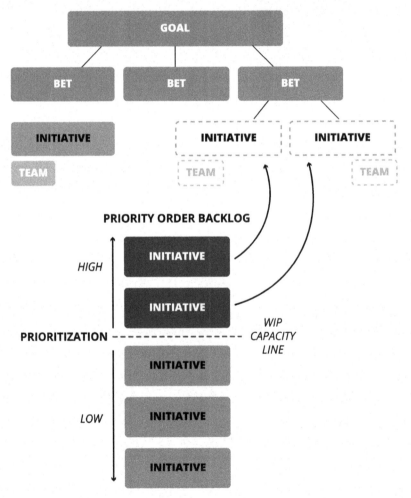

Periodic Value Review Dashboard

In a PVR, the portfolio owner team reviews the portfolio for the previous period, illustrating the deliveries made, the value produced (MoS), the investments made, and the work in progress, and providing a glimpse into what's on the top of the backlog. This is a complete picture of the portfolio that's intended to provide enough information to support a value-based conversation between the stakeholders and the team responsible for delivery of value from the portfolio. Figure 8-5 is an example dashboard that consolidates this information on a single page.

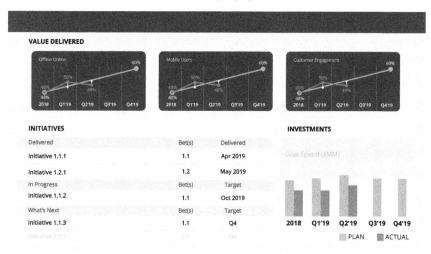

Figure 8-5
Example of an EDGE dashboard for PVR.

Final Thoughts

The term "lightweight governance" should in no way be interpreted as less important governance. However, it is another one of those areas where bureaucracy and excessive documentation tend to grow over time. Governance is critical to organizations. You leave yourself open to big problems if governance is done poorly. But just as agile software development has shown that much of the bureaucracy was unnecessary, so you can streamline your approach to governance to meet the demands of today's fast-moving environment. Meeting customer value, regulatory, financial, and safety goals is still core to your management responsibilities.

Chapter 9

Autonomous Teams and Collaborative Decision Making

You can't work alone anymore—the world is too complex. No one person, or even a single functional group, within an organization has sufficient knowledge or experience to plan and implement even a small digital initiative. You need a team of people to accomplish your digital goals—but what kind of team do you need? As you will read in this chapter, you need a team that has the following characteristics:

- Autonomous
- Self-sufficient in both knowledge and perspectives
- Collaborative
- Decisive
- Aligned to product and business capability

You Are Not Alone

Of course, a group can have all of these characteristics and still not be the elusive "jelled" team that Tom DeMarco and Tim Lister wrote about more than 30 years ago in one of the best ever books on teamwork.[1]

---

1. DeMarco, Tom, and Tim Lister. *Peopleware: Productive Projects and Teams.* New York: Dorset House, 1987.

Whether teams jell or not is based on that elusive "chemistry" among people. Some teams appear to have the right ingredients to work—but don't. Some teams seem to be lacking ingredients needed to succeed—but do. If one of the hundreds of authors of books on teams had the answer to this conundrum, we could just refer you to that source. Unfortunately, that singular solution doesn't exist, so the team topics in this chapter cover characteristics you might consider when building your teams, at all levels, to compete in today's world. Good luck!

Think back to Figure 1-3 and the opportunity/capability gap. Thanks to your development of a Lean Value Tree (LVT) and Measures of Success (MoS), there is now an air of excitement about the future. You have zeroed in on goals; now comes implementation, building the products and capabilities required. We are reminded of Jerry Weinberg's admonition, "No matter how it looks at first, it's always a people problem."[2] This chapter focuses on a subset of the "people problem" or, as we prefer to phrase it, a "people opportunity"—the "How should people work together in teams?" question. Putting people together into teams isn't enough. Putting people together into self-sufficient teams isn't enough. Empowering teams isn't enough. Part of the answer to the core question of how we should work together is that we must build innovative, quick-responding, value-driven, learning, high-performance teams.

Autonomous Teams

EDGE is similar to the agile and lean approaches in its use and promotion of effective teams. A number of concepts have been attached to our modern teams—autonomous, collaborative, self-sufficient.

Fundamentally, autonomous teams have both the authority and the accountability to deliver an outcome-oriented work product—whether that is a software feature (code) or a prioritized portfolio that implements a goal. A collaborative team is jointly accountable for results—everyone

2. Weinberg, Gerald M. *The Secrets of Consulting*. New York: Dorset House Publishing, 1985.

contributes. A self-sufficient team contains a variety of capabilities and diversity of perspectives needed to produce results with minimal dependencies on other teams or individuals. Work needs to be organized by the team's own specific outcomes. Each outcome should be owned by one team, rather than being divided across several teams. A team owns an outcome, not a fixed piece of code or technology.

Why Autonomous Teams?

Autonomous teams have the principles and capabilities needed to deliver a unit of value. This allows them to resolve the challenges that result from having work spread across multiple teams.

Autonomous teams benefit from the following characteristics:

- **Reduced dependencies.** Handoffs create delays, lowering quality and separating work from its business goals, as features cascade through multiple teams.
- **Increased throughput.** Reducing dependencies and the number of handoffs required to complete a piece of work increases throughput.
- **Simplified work estimation.** Removing the scheduling and sequencing of work across teams reduces complexity in estimating when work will be complete.
- **Improved transparency.** Progress of work and available capacity across the entire system are clearly visible.
- **Improved alignment to vision.** Aligning teams to measurable value and the big-picture vision reduces the risk of wandering off course.
- **Grit.** When unforeseen consequences and priorities change, teams have the endurance to quickly respond to change.
- **Risk reduction.** In uncertain, volatile environments, the greatest risk is utilizing traditional functional teams and hierarchical management: They don't encourage either innovation or speed.

Management authors have often used three related terms over the years—delegation, empowerment, and autonomy. The first term, delegation, speaks to assignment of tasks to another person or team. The concept of delegation has been a management staple since the early 20th century. Delegation has come to be more about tasks than about decisions. A manager assigns work by delegating to someone, but the ultimate accountability for results remains with the delegator. In the view of Frederick Winslow Taylor (the famous early 20th century management theorist and author of *The Principles of Scientific Management*[3]), workers were like cogs in a machine. They were given—delegated—a task to do and detailed instructions for accomplishing that task.

In today's uncertain and knowledge-driven world, you need exactly the opposite premise about people and work. This opposite approach is illustrated in Daniel Pink's *Drive: The Surprising Truth about What Motivates Us.*[4] Pink stresses that three essential components in engaging employees are autonomy, mastery, and purpose. Where delegation is about tasks, autonomy is about decisions.

> *To delegate means to choose or elect a person to act as a representative for another. To empower someone means to give power or authority to someone else. Do you hear the difference? To delegate something to someone is to only give them enough leash to act on your behalf, as you would for yourself. To empower another means you give them enough power and authority to act on their own behalf. ... To truly empower someone you must grant them authority, you must give them proper resources, and you must hold them accountable to organizational values and principles. They have to have enough authority to make some significant and important decisions.*[5]

Some people—Pink, for example—think that empowerment, as practiced, doesn't go far enough, as authority is dribbled out to employees by

3. Taylor, Frederick Winslow. *The Principles of Scientific Management.* Martino Fine Books, 2014 (original in 1911).
4. Pink, Daniel H. *Drive: The Surprising Truth about What Motivates Us.* New York: Riverhead Books, 2009.
5. Runn, Gary. "Delegation vs Empowerment." Gary Runn [blog], September 6, 2010. http://garyrunn.com/2010/09/06/delegation-vs-empowerment/.

management. So we will make this explicit differentiation between empowerment and autonomy. Empowered teams have only the decision-making power assigned to them by management. Autonomous teams have decision-making power over everything *except* that retained explicitly by management. This is a big difference. We will use the term "autonomy" because it suggests both a wider range of team self-governance and a sense of innate power rather than delegated power.[6]

You can measure autonomy by the degree of self-governance and independence. Autonomous teams are self-directed, with clear goals and boundaries they can work within. Within an organization, teams cannot be completely independent, but they do need to have a degree of control or autonomy over their immediate work environment to fully engage in that work. With freedom comes accountability—assuming the responsibilities for actions, decisions, deliverables, and disclosing results. To be autonomous, teams have to be accountable. So, how much autonomy is beneficial? Is more better? Until when? When does autonomy slide into anarchy? How do you balance autonomy with accountability?

Autonomous teams should work toward assigned customer value outcomes, rather than being assigned tasks. What to work on is, generally, given to the team through the prioritization of initiatives in the LVT and the backlog. The team, which should include a product person, collaboratively prioritizes what it will work on during the next iteration to deliver on the outcomes assigned to the team. How the team accomplishes the outcome should be determined by the team. However, in the realm of how teams work, the degree of autonomy isn't an absolute.

The two things assigned to teams from leaders are outcomes and boundaries. The first defines what the teams are accountable for; the second identifies the constraints on the teams. Chapter 5, Measuring and Prioritizing Value, discussed guardrail MoS. These measures act as one set of boundaries for delivery teams. Wide boundaries lead to greater autonomy, whereas narrow boundaries don't. For example, how much leeway does a software delivery team have in determining which tools it can use? Do the members

---

6. This is sometimes called "powers reserved," and it is very similar to the concept outlined in the U.S. Constitution. People have rights inherently; they are not granted. Also, states have all powers not explicitly granted to the federal government, as opposed to having only what the federal government grants them (the states).

have choices in some areas (languages) but not in others (continuous integration)? Which choices do they have in conforming to architectural standards? As the software stack for any development effort has exploded over the last 10-plus years,[7] organizations with strict tool standards have been at a distinct disadvantage, as their process for adding new tools has been too slow to take advantage of rapid advances.[8] So too little leeway may stunt innovation—but will too much lead to confusion and inefficiency?

One way to approach these questions is to go back to a basic principle emphasized in this book—operating at the edge of chaos to foster innovation and creativity. Operating at the edge means putting some structure in place, but not too much. The edge is sharp, so people try to stay away from it—gravitating to either too much or too little structure. Balancing at the edge is difficult to define; it's more of a judgment call. For leaders and managers used to prescriptive processes and practices, the judgment call around the comment "It depends" can be difficult to digest.

Team Composition: From Cross-Functional to Self-Sufficient Teams

Since the early days of agile development (and before), practitioners have promoted the idea of cross-functional teams. IT team compositions often included developers, testers, analysts, and others. As agile practices evolved, roles such as product specialists and IT operations were included. In either case, some specialized skilled members were part time and designated as subject-matter experts (SMEs). These teams were called cross-functional because they drew needed skilled members from their functional organizations.

However, as explained in the section of this chapter on aligning organizations to business capability, agile organizations (not just IT) are moving toward an organizational structure driven by capabilities (internal) and

---

7. Highsmith, Jim, Mike Mason, and Neal Ford. "Implications of Tech Stack Complexity for Executives." *ThoughtWorks Insights*, December. 14, 2015. https://www.thoughtworks.com/insights/blog/implications-tech-stack-complexity-executives.
8. Just look back at the tech radar in Chapter 2, Tech@Core, to see the number of "new" items from the previous rendition.

products (external). Since these newer-style structures are not designed around functions, the term "cross-functional" loses its meaning. What you need today are teams with "sufficient" knowledge and skill to carry out their goals—whether those are technology or marketing skills.

Autonomous teams need to be as independent of other parts of the organization as possible. For example, traditional IT teams often were composed of analysts, programmers, project managers, testers, database specialists, and more. These members were often "matrixed," meaning they reported to functional managers (who dealt with personnel and performance matters). Team members usually (more likely, always) had more allegiance to their functional hierarchy than to their project teams. These matrix dependencies and lack of allegiance to project teams resulted in slow progress and poor quality because there was little accountability. The more dependencies you have, the more excuses you have to avoid that accountability. Self-sufficient teams are constructed to reduce these dependencies to the greatest extent possible.

A self-sufficient team should include all the capabilities necessary to deliver the work in its portfolio. A typical software delivery team may have between four and eight skill areas represented. Executive and leadership teams should have similar self-sufficiency—CIO, CFO, VP product development, VP marketing.

From Silos to Self-Sufficient Teams

We worked with a financial services company that had three functional silos—software developers, lawyers, and accountants—working on its mortgage industry software product. The regulations that covered the product line's financial transactions were different in every state, and the company also had to comply with federal regulations. The three functional areas were in different building locations, and "requirements" were transmitted in document form. Prioritization—from the portfolio level to the feature level—was based on the age-old principle of who shouted the loudest. Miscommunication and missed deadlines were rampant. Competitors launched innovative new products and services faster than our client could, and they were able to create better user experiences around legislative guidelines—things that were considered constraints by the client's in-house lawyers. Things needed to change.

One of the key changes that enabled this organization to deliver value sooner was to realign delivery into product-centric teams that included software developers, accountants, and lawyers. The software development group itself also reorganized into self-sufficient teams, where roles such as developer, tester, analyst, user experience specialist, and product manager were now assigned to product teams.

The results of the reorganization, and other process improvements, enabled the company to better prioritize higher-valued opportunities and products. Moreover, collaboration replaced detailed documentation, morale improved, and market-leading products were released on a more competitive schedule.

After operating with these new teams for a few months, the development director was asked how it was going. "Great," he said. "The product teams are communicating much better and delivery has improved. However, now the communications between product teams is suffering!"

Nothing solves all the problems: You just hope the problems that the solutions create are smaller than the problems they solve. In this case, since several products were sold to customers as a suite, the delivery teams needed to be cognizant of one another's work. Even so, the product orientation still solved more problems than it caused.

In EDGE, one of the major shifts in practice is from upfront detailed planning and analysis to more holistic long-term road mapping; this allows planning to be directionally consistent, yet responsive to new information. The big-picture view is needed to provide the structure to knit together a complex solution. It also provides a point of reference as new learning happens and the details of a plan or design need to be revised.

This shift in thinking represents a major change for individuals who have excelled using traditional practices, so it should be nurtured deliberately by leadership and the Value Realization Team (explained later in this chapter).

Trust Relationships

Collaboration is simply two or more individuals working together to create a product or share knowledge. The core of successful collaborative teams is trust. Indeed, trust lies at the heart of autonomy, collaboration, and effective decision making. If leaders don't fully trust their teams or if team members lack mutual trust, the result is performance degradation. Figure 9-1 shows the dimensions of interactions along a low to high trust line. We frequently think of these dimensions as existing in relationships among team members, but they also apply to the relationships between leaders/managers and teams that report to them.

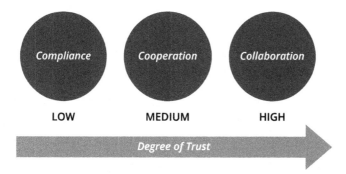

Figure 9-1
Three dimensions of interactions.

A good friend of Jim's once related a story about his 14-year old daughter, who was having a surly day. "It's your turn to put the dishes away," said the dad to the daughter after dinner. Later, the dad confronted the daughter: "Why did you put the *dirty* dishes away?" To which the daughter replied, "Dad, you said to put the dishes away; you didn't say to wash them first!"

This is a perfect example of compliance—performing an assigned task but taking no responsibility for the outcome. The daughter followed her instructions—to the letter—even though she knew it wasn't the outcome her dad desired. "Not my fault; I did what I was told to do." Compliance interactions have very little trust. Therefore, both parties try to protect themselves from "fault" by having a detailed agreement (in many cases, a contract) and following that agreement even when they know it won't produce the desired outcome. "Not my fault" is the oft-heard compliance mantra. In the *Dilbert* comic strip, Wally epitomizes a compliance mentality.

Cooperative interactions are in the middle: They have some trust that may be shaky and some accountability, but staff always keep an eye on a fallback position that deflects blame. Cooperative teams will go beyond written agreements, but they fall back on them when trouble looms.

A truly collaborative interaction begins with a high degree of trust that has been established over time. This level of trust can survive a few glitches. No human interactions, no matter the degree of trust, are glitchless. The secret is talking over the glitch and taking responsibility. A collaborative team takes full responsibility for delivering outcomes within established boundaries. They don't make excuses or blame individual team members.

Autonomous teams strive for the collaborative end of the spectrum. There needs to be collaborative relationships among team members and between the team and management. Autonomous teams do not arise from statements like "You are now an autonomous team," but rather from actions and interactions that build trust and accountability.

Accountability and Autonomy

Both managers and team members struggle with accountability and autonomy. Managers have a difficult time letting go of decision making. They are nervous about whether the team can make good decisions, given that the team members may not have the experience of the manager. They are concerned that the team members won't take accountability or their commitments seriously, or that the manager will be left holding the bag for the poor decisions if things go south. For their part, teams are concerned that managers won't give them enough autonomy, that they will say the words but won't let go in practice. Team members may also be concerned about being blamed for something they have no control over (what they don't realize is that few people are really in "control"). Teams worry that managers will make unreasonable commitments without discussing those commitments with them first.

Neither a team nor its managers become autonomous overnight. They have to build up a level of trust in each other so that their fears about each other are minimized. You could think of the progression using the forming–storming–norming–performing model of team development originated by Bruce Tuckman in the 1960s. Just as teams take time to jell, so the relationship between a team and its managers takes time to jell. But in this evolving relationship, trust (as defined in the last section) is paramount. The underlying cause of many of the struggles mentioned earlier is lack of trust. You might even think of the levels of trust (compliance, cooperation, and collaboration) as a rough correlation to Tuckman's model. In the beginning, the forming stage, there is little trust and everyone operates in the compliance mode. In the storming stage, people are trying to better understand and appreciate each other. The trust level may reach cooperation by the early stages of norming. By the end of norming and into the performing stage, trust has built to the true collaboration level, and both teams and their managers are performing. Of course, the evolution doesn't happen overnight; in fact, it may take weeks and even months.

While implementation strategies for building autonomous teams vary, we propose one practice that appears to speed the process: "Trust first." The tendency of managers is to tell their teams, either explicitly or implicitly, "As you prove that you will be accountable for results, I will give you more autonomy." At the same time the team members are thinking, "You are just talking about giving us autonomy. We're going to wait until we see it before we agree to be accountable." These behaviors slow down the adoption and performance of autonomous teams. The better solution is for the managers to believe, "I assume that you will be accountable for results until you prove otherwise. And, given that we are just starting on this journey, I also assume there will be some misfires, so I will give the team leeway until we all understand how this is going to work." Team members say, "We will assume a level of trust to begin with and work toward defining what autonomy means in our organization; in the meantime, we will do our best to hold ourselves accountable for results we have committed to." This second set of comments basically says, "We are going to trust each other first."

With Autonomy Comes Accountability

We were working with a financial services company team that was implementing agile practices and learning in an effort to become more autonomous and accountable. During an iteration planning session, the product management VP came in briefly and stressed the need to complete certain stories in the iteration to be prepared for an important customer demonstration. After the VP left, the team analyzed the stories and agreed that they could complete them; they reported their plans to the VP and their manager. They ran into obstacles at the end of the first week of the two-week iteration. Although they worked hard during the second week, they came up just short of their story goals.

The VP was disappointed, and so was their manager, especially after a debriefing with the team at which he learned that during the second week the team members left work at the normal 5 p.m. time. With a few hours of overtime, they could have completed the stories. While working overtime on a regular basis isn't recommended (although in many companies it is still the norm), in this case the team didn't live up to their commitment. They should have agreed within the team to commit a few extra hours to complete the stories. Part of being accountable is delivering on commitments you have made if at all possible. This incident damaged their relationship with the VP and reduced the trust level between the team and their manager.

Of course, there are many facets to this issue. If we assume estimates will always be wrong, then teams will always work late—unless they start padding their estimates, which we don't want them to do because we hope management trusts them. So, there should be a safe place to say, "Our estimates are wrong," and collaboration between the team and the manager to decide on a path forward. One path might be to work extra hours, but it's not the only option.

Creating an Environment That Fosters Autonomy

Leaders can take a number of actions to foster autonomy, such as having teams set their own schedule, decide what to work on and who works on it, make their own make-or-buy decisions, and integrate their work with other teams. In *Drive,* Daniel Pink discusses a company that practices ROWE—a results-only work environment. In this company, employees set their own work hours—completely. It doesn't matter when or where you work, as long as you get results. However, you might ask about coordination meetings with other teams: How do you schedule them if every team is on a different schedule?

There might be a couple of solutions to this question. One would be to set common hours (say, 10 a.m. to 3 p.m.) when everyone should be at the office for such meetings. Or, given that the teams are committed to their assigned outcomes, you could leave it up to them (trust them) to figure out how to accomplish the needed coordination.

Creating an environment that encourages autonomy requires exceptional leadership—particularly in making the transition from traditional teams. In the beginning, some teams will not want either the authority or the accountability—because to a greater or lesser extent they don't trust their leaders. They fear accountability without authority. Leaders, in contrast, fear losing control and that teams will make unwise decisions or will shirk accountability. The processes and practices of EDGE may be the easiest to implement in an organization; autonomous teams and adaptive leadership may prove more difficult.

EDGE Teams

How we work together begins with how we organize. Hierarchical organizations with slow decision making won't survive—but neither will working alone. The agile/lean world is built around autonomous, self-sufficient teams (which are core EDGE principles). This is one of the ways in which EDGE goes beyond portfolio management and moves into the realm of an operating model. It's not enough to invest wisely in innovation; you have to manage these initiatives differently, whether at the delivery team or at the executive team level.

When moving to EDGE, organizational structures and roles need to be in alignment with the organizational goals. Self-sufficient teams, whose members are domain experts, ensure that all perspectives are represented, so good decisions can be made as quickly as possible. Multiple perspectives improve the odds that innovative solutions will also be practical and workable.

EDGE's operating model trusts teams to make smart choices, based on the business goals, financial constraints, and learning experienced throughout development. For individuals, this requires holistic thinking at all levels of the portfolio (goal, bet, initiative). Organizationally, it means teams are long-lived and aligned with a business capability or product. This can be a big change for traditional organizations, which tend to be organized along functions such as marketing, inventory management, information technology, and product development.

The Value Realization Team

The Value Realization Team (VRT),which replaces a Project or Portfolio Management Office (PMO), plays a key role in change by supporting the right kind of new organization, helping the current organization migrate gradually to the new one, and providing ongoing coaching and mentoring. The VRT is not a control-oriented organization like the traditional PMO, but rather a consultative and facilitative one. "Why make the switch from PMO to VRT?" you might ask. If you are just changing the name but keeping the same activities, there isn't a need to change. However, if you are trying to change the culture so that it focuses on facilitation rather than control, a new name can help bridge that gap—it can turn the constraints of existing governance processes into helpful supporting behaviors.

The VRT focuses on accelerating the delivery of value. It has primary responsibility for facilitating the EDGE processes, maintaining the integrity of the EDGE methods and artifacts, and coaching and mentoring people in developing a continuous learning mindset. Ultimately, the power to "fix things" resides with the portfolio owners and delivery teams.

The Role of the VRT

- Support agile/lean practices and a continuous learning mindset
- Facilitate the review and adjustment of investments
- Facilitate the work intake process
- Share investment landscape visualization
- Share resource engagement visualization
- Share performance measurements
- Foster communities of practice
- Facilitate pivoting or stopping of investments
- Facilitate new goals, bets, and initiatives

The VRT is typically smaller than a traditional PMO and is primarily staffed by coaches, facilitators, and analysts. The overall intent when establishing such a team is to resolve systemic organization-wide challenges and to lighten the burden on teams and leaders while maintaining sufficient governance.

Governance and reporting should be both lightweight and effective. The VRT helps teams develop reports that are meaningful, quick to construct, and built into the way teams do delivery. To protect the integrity of EDGE, the VRT also checks that prioritization is done consistently, that investment allocation is revisited in a disciplined and regular way, and that people are following through with their leadership and ownership duties.

One challenge with mixed skill teams is that members need a means of support, career development, and skills sharing. The VRT helps foster communities of practice (CoP), a type of cross-cutting affinity group that links the practitioners in a domain (business: marketing, finance, operations; or IT: user experience, product specialists developers) to others with an interest in the field. The VRT should not run these CoPs, but the team members can provide both guidance and nurturing to the communities and their leaders.

The VRT should ensure that the current state of investment be easily accessed by looking at information radiators. Resource allocation and progress should be visible. This includes sharing what bet and initiative teams are working on and which teams have additional capacity.

Portfolio Teams

We often think about delivery teams at the level of producing software code, but fail to think about teams at every level—from vision to delivery. In EDGE, the processes and practices are fractal in that they are similar at every level, but may operate on different artifacts. For example, an executive team determines goals and priorities, whereas a delivery team determines small slices of business functionality and their priority—but the processes and practices are basically the same. Every EDGE team type, from executive to delivery, needs to be collaborative, self-sufficient, and autonomous.

A few definitions, or distinctions, are in order. You don't want to say "goal, bet, and initiative team" (too unwieldy) every time you talk about teams, so the generic term for one or all of these types of teams will be "portfolio team." A goal team may also be called an executive team, and an initiative team is also a delivery team (a delivery team's portfolio is more often referred to as a backlog). It is important to note that the same individual may serve on multiple levels of portfolio teams. The "teams" at each level are filled by roles. In smaller organizations, one individual might fulfill several roles at multiple levels; in larger organizations, there might be one person per role.

The "boxes" on the LVT are strategic outcomes. Each needs a multidisciplinary portfolio team to shape and direct it. It's not the job of the executive team or the VRT to define the approach taken to realize aspirations in each box. Instead, the portfolio teams take a target business outcome and determine how best to bring it about.

The portfolio teams collaboratively develop a robust vision of which drivers, constraints, and opportunities exist in their domain. They're responsible for defining outcomes, creating the solution, and delivering on the approach. For a portfolio team to benefit over time from learning, shared insights, and growing relationships, members should stay together. The strategic formulation of solution and approach is an intimate collaboration that matures over time and benefits from consistency. When a portfolio team is shared across several initiatives, it should be kept intact. For example, a product owner working on two bets should work with the same technical team on both, rather than having to adapt to an entirely new team.

> ### Summary of Use of the Term "Teams"
>
> #### Portfolio team
> The umbrella term for either a goal, bet, or initiative team.
>
> #### Goal team
> A self-sufficient group of leaders representing areas such as technology, user experience, product, manufacturing, operations, and marketing, who are accountable for the outcomes of the goal.
>
> #### Bet team
> A self-sufficient group of leaders representing areas such as technology, user experience, product, operations, and relevant business organizations, who are accountable for the outcomes of the bet.
>
> #### Initiative team
> A self-sufficient delivery team made up of roles such as developers, designers, product, architects, legal, marketing, and testing; also known as a delivery or product team.

Executive or Goal Teams

The executive or goal team develops an overall vision (in collaboration with other leaders), shapes the LVT message, and broadly allocates investments to goals (and multiple portfolios in the case of large organizations). This team should include your organization's senior strategic visionaries and include both business people and technologists.

The executive team actively shapes the high-level strategy; the members are not just "approvers" for plans developed by staff. It's essential that the team has direct engagement from senior leaders but not control over design and delivery. The executive team should guide other teams by clearly articulating actionable goals that can be achieved, and should choose where funding is allocated.

The executive or goal team steers the organization toward the achievement of the goals by setting MoS that align to value. It is then up to the bet and initiative teams to define how to achieve the goals using the measures as guidance.

Bet Team

Chapter 4, Building a Value-Driven Portfolio, introduced the term "bet" to emphasize the need to experiment rather than plan your way into the future. The bet team defines the critical link between goals that are high-level aspirations about the future and specific chunks of the desired outcomes. A bet team should include self-sufficient members, just as is true for other teams. The composition of these teams also needs to include personnel who have experience and interest in innovation, experimentation, and getting good feedback.

Initiative or Delivery Teams

Initiative or delivery teams should include members with all the principal capabilities needed to deliver an initiative (such as working software). A team owns a business outcome, not a fixed piece of code or technology. It should include both product and technology roles. Some roles may not require full-time participation in the team (e.g., legal, operations, security), so the people playing these roles can serve more than one team simultaneously. In such cases, they should serve in the same bet or goal branch for focus and alignment. Be careful not to spread them too thin.

Self-Sufficient Collaboration Leads to Better Outcomes

We were working with a retail organization that wanted to replace a legacy system used in its head office. In the old way of working, product and user experience designs were created up front, approved, and shipped off to the development team. The development team would assess the designs and estimate the effort required to build the product. The product team would take all this information and request funding—which would always be much less than requested. The team would then spend long hours in meetings deciding on what to de-scope, compromising on features until they had a scope within the budget allocated.

In the new way of working, a team of self-sufficient leaders (user experience, technology, process and product) was empowered to create a vision for the product that included the desired user experience, business viability, and technical feasibility of the product. This working model was named "four in the box" to describe the diverse opinions needed to define a product that could be delivered incrementally, with value realized in weeks, rather than months or years.

Through the process of product discovery, we found that consumer needs were changing, creating demand for mobile access to vital data to make better business decisions. We were able to identify a greater opportunity to make existing data available through a mobile device, which facilitated faster decisions for customers and delivered earlier realization of customer value. This moved the decision from "How much budget is needed to replace a legacy system?" to "How fast can we deliver value to customers and shift away from building feature parity?" To work in this new way, the company needed the diverse knowledge of product, user experience, technology, and process to come together to co-create a solution that was far better than the one users previously had.

Collaborative, Self-Sufficient Decisions

Most decision making in today's organizations is done in one of two ways:

1. A single individual is given decision rights for a particular domain, and all decisions are channeled through this person. This approach will often minimize the time necessary to actually make the decision because no discussion is needed. However, sometimes these decision makers can become a bottleneck in the system, as decisions get queued up waiting to be made. A failure mode for this decision process is using the decision rights as a club in the rough and tumble politics of today's organizations.

2. A group is assembled to make the decision. Often the group membership is based on who is interested in a topic, or available, or willing to do it. Group decisions tend to take longer to make because the group has to debate/discuss the subject. Sometimes the decisions get delayed because members of the group are not available or they get stuck in analysis paralysis. Failure mode for this process is compromise behavior, in which the decision devolves to what everyone in the group can live with. On a positive note, the decision quality is often improved because the collective wisdom of the group is greater than the wisdom of a single individual.

You want teams to have autonomy to think creatively and make decisions that they believe to be the right ones. But you also want to grow your leaders so that they know when to step in and steer teams in a positive direction when necessary. Decision-making people and processes need to balance responsiveness with decision quality. The people factor is partly about choosing how many people are involved, and partly about the decision process used. A well-run process with more people could beat a poorly run one with a few people and could be speedier. Similarly, a large group of unprepared people who have no stake in the outcome (or have competing objectives) don't necessarily make a better-quality decision than a single individual who's responsible for the decision.

Autonomous teams have significant decision-making latitude. So the next question becomes "How do these teams make 'good' decisions?" The title of this section identifies two key aspects of good team decision making: self-sufficient expertise and collaboration.

Slow Decisions

A number of years ago, Jim was consulting with a software company in Dublin, Ireland. Management was concerned that the development staff was too slow and wanted improvement suggestions. After talking with a number of managers, team leads, and developers, Jim determined that the problem was not slow developers, but rather slow management decisions. Every time a product decision needed to be made, even a fairly low-level decision, the development teams had to refer the decisions to the headquarters staff in Silicon Valley. Because the headquarters staff had their own set of priorities and didn't have daily contact with the staff in Ireland, even minor decisions often took weeks—leading to much frustration in the dev team. This situation prompted comments like, "It seems that they don't care, so why should we," which obviously led to even slower progress.

Jim's recommendation to the group and their management was to (1) gather data on the time delays for their requests, (2) based on that data to establish new processes such that requests had higher priority with the HQ group, and (3) empower the Ireland office staff to make more day-to-day decisions on their own. These recommendations were implemented reasonably quickly and led to faster decision turnaround, faster feature delivery, and improved morale in the dev team.

The preceding story illustrates a few of the factors that go into good group decisions:

- You need individuals with self-sufficient knowledge.
- You need diverse social perspectives.
- You need trust and respect among the participants.
- You need participants who are open to others' ideas.
- You need facilitators who are adept at encouraging wide participation.
- You need participants who are willing to participate.

Self-Sufficient Knowledge

Building self-sufficient teams is much more difficult than assembling people with different skills into teams: It requires management attention throughout the organization. For example, commingling technical and business people is a challenge—as illustrated by the tension between meeting business goals, meeting customer needs, and utilizing good technical practices within the constraints of time, cost, and quality. Practitioners of extreme programming advocated a number of technical practices such as refactoring and pair programming. Scrum practitioners, by contrast, started with sprint planning and daily stand-up meetings. Ardent agile practitioners voice concerns that the technical practices of agile are undervalued in many agile implementations. This often heated debate within the agile community itself illustrates the difficulty of melding the disparate views of people from technical and business backgrounds into a coherent whole. Organizations that have figured how to balance and integrate these two aspects have been the most successful.

Self-sufficient teams should have the knowledge and skills to deliver a product. However, sometimes these teams require specialized knowledge for a short period of time. In this case, how far do you go with self-sufficiency on a team? It depends on dependencies. You want wide enough self-sufficiency and decision-making power that teams minimize dependencies on other functional areas or teams. Think of traditional organizations in which business analysts, developers, testers, and operations staff operate in separate functional teams. These teams are dependent on each other at a very low level. Even though they may be working toward the same goal, they will inevitably have different priorities. They will also have different processes and performance metrics that focus more on functional success than on outcome success. With this structure, you go as far as you can in reducing dependencies without creating more inefficiency than it's worth. At the extreme, there would be zero dependencies (a fully autonomous team), but this approach often under-utilizes specialty resources such as security because you don't need them all the time.

We have seen far too many instances where the business analysts, developers, testers, and operations groups are at odds with each other, with their conflicts exacerbated by functional performance metrics that operate against producing desired outcomes. In one case, the business analysis group's performance was measured, in part, by delivery of a "complete" specification document on time. This group inevitably had little time to actually talk to the development team. Furthermore, once the document was "completed," the business analysts were reluctant to change it. By contrast, the goals with self-sufficient teams are to minimize dependencies and to maximize mutual commitment to outcomes.

Diverse Social Perspectives

Self-sufficient knowledge isn't sufficient—you also need diverse perspectives. As every management consultant and author points out, the world is shrinking and companies need social perspectives that include diversities based on region, country, race, gender, religion, sexual orientation, and more.

Diversity Improves Team Decision Making

Teams make better decisions than individuals do 66 percent of the time.

All-male teams make better decisions 58 percent of the time.

Age + gender + geographic–diverse teams make better decisions 87 percent of the time.

—Study by Cloverpop, "Hacking Diversity with Inclusive Decision Making," www.cloverpop.com

---

As of early 2019, ThoughtWorks had more than 5000 employees in 14 countries. When working for multinational clients, it is important—no, critical—to bring global perspectives from China, India, Europe, North America, Australia, Brazil, and others to engagements. Doing so may take extra time, and it may be frustrating at times. Even so, bringing diverse social perspectives to your digital transformation is critically important to self-sufficient knowledge.

Some may argue that perspectives based on characteristics such as age or sexual orientation have no place in a business setting. We don't agree. People spend a significant part of their lives working, so all of these perspectives have great relevance. As many companies have shown, valuing these perspectives can lead to positive social change.

Trust and Respect

For a team to be effective, it needs both trust and respect. Respect entails accepting, and even admiring, that others have the requisite knowledge and experience to contribute to the team. Trust is the belief in the reliability of others, believing that they will, to the best of their ability, do what they commit to doing.

In our tech-driven world, tech skills, knowledge, and capabilities are critical—and often lead to a tech-centric meritocracy in organizations.

A potential downside of this meritocracy is a lack of respect for "others." Developers may disrespect testers. Project managers may disrespect developers. Technologists may disrespect product management. Hardware teams may disrespect software teams. Delivery teams may disrespect management.

Some rivalry between groups is healthy, but disrespect is detrimental to collaboration. Jim once facilitated an off-site design session for a new medical instrument. At one point, several of the hardware engineers made a disrespectful comment about software developers. Called out on his comment, one engineer sheepishly said, "Oh, we weren't talking about the software developers on our team; we were referring to the group back at the office."

Respect doesn't necessarily imply that all team members contribute equally to success. On basketball teams, for example, there are stars—like Lebron James—and role players. Without the role players, the stars won't succeed, but everyone understands that the stars may determine ultimate success. On good teams, there is mutual respect among all the players, even as they recognize the differing contributions of various members. Everyone contributes and is part of the win.

Open to Others' Ideas

Innovation begins with openness to ideas, even the bad ones. Openness is closely tied to trust and respect, as it is difficult to be open when these behaviors are missing. Team members need a fundamental belief that ideas can progress from good to better to best by integrating multiple perspectives into a final product.

Allowing Diverse Perspectives to Be Heard

Years ago, Jim was facilitating a design meeting at a major airline. At some point, the group made a tentative decision with a vote of 14–1. A typical group would have moved on with such an overwhelming vote. In this case, one person in the group asked the lone holdout, a quiet individual who hadn't said much, why he cast a dissenting vote. It turned out that he had domain knowledge and experience that no one else had. By the time he finished talking, he had convinced everyone else that he was correct and the vote was reversed to 0–15.

We once worked with a team in which one member was always bringing up multiple reasons why someone else's idea wouldn't work. This member, who was very knowledgeable about his subject area, was very astute at generating problems with new ideas. This, of course, put a damper on other team members' willingness to voice their ideas. One day we approached this naysayer with a challenge: "Today, we don't want you to say anything about why ideas won't work. We want you to only voice your own ideas to address the issues." He couldn't do it! It made him realize how difficult it was to think up new ideas and he thereafter tempered his negative comments.

It's not that you want to ignore issues with ideas, but rather that you need to encourage multiple ideas and then later subject them to practical implementation discussions. Intentional processes can also help brainstorming sessions—for example, separating idea generation from idea analysis.

Facilitators

To be effective, every self-sufficient team needs one or more skilled facilitators. Teams hold many different types of get-togethers: daily stand-ups, brainstorming, retrospectives, showcases,[9] and more. Some types of meetings, especially those with larger groups of people, require greater facilitation skills. Ideally, some volunteers from the team will be interested in gaining or enhancing these skills. They will keep everyone involved, keep meetings on track, and nudge participants into making good decisions. A good facilitator can mean the difference between boring, unfruitful meetings that go on and on, and meetings that produce results in a timely manner and leave the participants energized. Good facilitators help turn groups of people into jelled teams. Having people with the right self-sufficient skills and experience on a team isn't enough—you need someone to tie them together. Every self-sufficient team needs members with facilitation skills.

Slow Decision Making

An oft-quoted problem raised about collaborative decisions is that making them is too slow—too much talking, not enough deciding. While this can

---

9. A showcase is an end-of-iteration presentation of a working application to the clients or customers.

be an issue, good teams know that the process can actually be considerably faster:

- Some decisions can be made by subsets of the full team, or even by the leaders.
- When everyone has participated in the decision, they are likely to be more committed to its implementation.
- Slow decision making is often the result of poor understanding of the goals or MoS of the initiative.
- Slow decision making is often the result of poor facilitation.

When people complain about slow team decisions, they are generally thinking about one-off decisions, not a series of decisions that the team needs to make. Good teams accelerate the process from one decision to the next by carrying forward a good understanding of the goals, bets, MoS, and other contextual information. They don't have to rehash the meaning of the goals or other items. The discussion of these items may take more time in the beginning until the entire team becomes comfortable with their understanding, but little time thereafter. If the team continues to debate goals and other underlying precepts, it is a strong indication that something is wrong. It is similar to the issue with some agile teams when they get lost in the details of weekly iterations and lose track of their outcome goals.

In teams that are not self-sufficient or co-located, it may take days or even weeks to find time to meet and make decisions. Agile teams, which are usually co-located either physically or electronically, can use daily stand-up meetings to make minor decisions on the spot, or convene meetings quickly to discuss more consequential decisions. Furthermore, on more traditional teams in which members don't work together in close proximity, those members often don't know each other very well, so their decision making takes more time as they try to understand each other's positions.

Willingness to Participate

How many times have you worked in a team in which one or more members tended to sit in the corner, working away by themselves? These same individuals are reluctant to attend meetings or group discussions. Granted, everyone needs alone time, but that is different from unwillingness to participate. We once worked with a client whose developers had individual offices and where a knock on the door with an inquiry like "Can I ask you a quick question?" was often met by the response "Send me an email." This was a company in which technical meritocracy was embedded in the culture and staff had little incentive to interact with others. This was a very successful company for a lengthy time—but its innovation also suffered over that span.

Having individuals who participate fully in the team can determine the level of success. But there can also be over-participation—excessive meetings that drain the members' enthusiasm for team activities. As in other areas, balancing rules the day, again.

Aligning Organizations to Business Capability

An LVT is aligned around outcomes of customer value at every level. Traditionally, many business and technical organizations have been organized around functions. For example, at the IT delivery team level (initiative), organizational structure was often functional—developers, testers, designers, database specialists, and more. Individuals in each of these groups tended to work part time on project teams, but they identified more with their functional areas than with the teams. Project teams tended to remain together only for the duration of the project. The functional breakdowns in IT mirrored the stages in a waterfall or serial approach to software development.

Having an LVT aligned around outcomes and an organization aligned around functions is a misalignment of people to desired outcomes. Depending on the maturity of your organization's agile practices, you may have broken down some of the silos: Developers, quality assurance testers, and analysts/product people may already be on the project teams simultaneously. If your organization has embraced continuous deployment and evolutionary architecture, enterprise architects and delivery infrastructure teams may already be working in concert with the team as well. Figure 9-2 shows self-sufficient teams at each level of the LVT structure.

Figure 9-2

Example of self-sufficient
portfolio teams at each
level in the Lean Value
Tree.

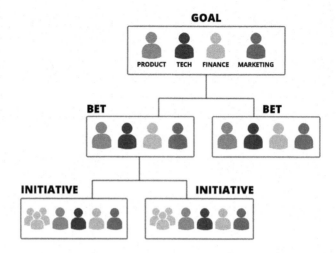

As organizations become customer-centric, marketing and design functions begin to play a focused and crucial part of the cross-team collaboration needed to effectively balance the demands of the business, the needs of the customer, and the technical practices needed to build great products. Thus, in your new organization, you want to:

- Institutionalize and expand self-sufficient teams to be longer-lived teams aligned on product or business capability.
- Expand lean concepts into the business by increasing business involvement in portfolio teams.

The first significant transition for organizations was from functional to self-sufficient teams, although in the beginning many agile teams[10] were limited to technical roles. From the earliest stages of agile software development, proponents recommended cross-functional (now self-sufficient) teams. Perhaps they tended to focus on stories (user requirements), which were written in business terms, but the early agile teams didn't focus on outcomes. The agile projects were often managed by traditional project management practices, including measuring conformance to scope, schedule, and cost plans. While these agile teams offered improved performance over

10. Non-agile teams also went through this transition from functional teams to cross-functional teams.

traditional development approaches, there was still much room for growth, as they improved on delivering stuff, but often did not deliver the *right* stuff.

The second transition in changing organizational alignment was from a project orientation to a product orientation, as shown in Figure 9-3.[11] This step expanded the skill areas included in the project team—most notably including product and tech operations staff. Agile teams began thinking about delivering and prioritizing stories using customer value. The technology organizations began switching from a project hierarchy to a product hierarchy in which product teams tended to remain together far longer than project teams did. The alignment between outcomes and organization improved, but there was still more to accomplish—including increasing business participation and eventually realigning business organizations. As organizations became customer-centric, marketing and design functions also played a focused and crucial part of the cross-team collaboration needed to effectively balance the demands of the business, the needs of the customer, and the technical practices required to build great products.

FROM...	TO...	OR TO...
Tech teams that form to carry out short-duration projects with a focus on delivering within the time, cost, and quality constraints set by stakeholders	Product teams that have self-sufficient product/tech/ops teams that deliver customer value	Capability teams that have self-sufficient tech/product/ops/ business teams that focus on delivering business value

Figure 9-3
The evolution of aligning organizations to product or business capabilities to derive the maximum value from investment in teams.

The third type of transition has been from project to capability, as organizations commit to outcome goals. This realignment includes both technology and business areas of the organization. This typically happens as organizations become customer driven from the outside in, rather than from the inside out. Desired customer value outcomes are then supported by business and technology capabilities, rather than by functions.

Business capabilities for an online retail company might be, for example, order processing, merchandising, catalog management, and customer billing. Unless the business changes significantly, these capabilities will

11. Public-sector organizations such as government and nonprofit organizations may want to substitute the term "client service" for "product."

be required for a very long time. Because a retail firm will always have a merchandising capability, it will therefore always need support and expansion of those digital assets. This logically leads to long-term technology and business groups dedicated to supporting this capability—from the executives to the delivery level. Another example would be the function of inventory management versus the business capability of order fulfilment. Fulfilling an order requires a number of business functions, such as inventory control, accounting, and shipping.

The big shift for organizations is to move from "part-time" transient project assignments of people, to dedicated longer-term product and business capability area assignments. That needn't mean people are stuck; it just means teams need to focus on a product/capability area. People can certainly move around, but in a responsible way. Roles must be backfilled and time must be given for people to get up to speed when they enter a new domain.

We prefer long-lived product/business capability teams to shepherd initiatives and the assets in their area, so that they not only create and deploy something but also support it. This encourages responsible tech debt management and quality practices. It also allows teams to sunset assets more quickly, thereby saving money and support time. Being responsible over the long haul reinforces the types of behavior that build value continuously.

A mix of product and capability alignment will be evident in many organizations, particularly software product companies. Software companies may choose to have a product alignment for their products, maintaining a customer value fitness function and a capability alignment for internal applications.

The end goal of these realignments is to have long-term teams of technology staff supporting product/business capabilities and measuring success based on achieving desired customer value outcomes. You probably won't reach this lofty goal in every part of your business—but successful digital enterprises will increasingly embrace this type of alignment.

Final Thoughts

In EDGE, we have been pursuing three key questions: (1) How should we invest?, (2) How can we adapt fast enough?, and (3) How should we work together? You might have an incredibly sophisticated portfolio investment process, but without the right organizational changes, your portfolio plans will expire on the petard of execution.

This book isn't about the normal course of business: It's about digital transformation, which means innovation, creativity, and speed. You won't achieve these results without the trio of autonomous teams, collaborative working and decision making, and the cultural changes outlined in Chapter 10, Adaptive Leadership. Answering the question of how you work together will drive the continuing success of your digital transformation.

Adaptive Leadership

One of the key questions that this book proposed to answer was "How can we adapt fast enough?" Fast enough today is different from what it was five years ago. Surviving and thriving while change accelerates requires a leadership culture built on responding to change over anything else. Whether you are responding to new opportunities or reacting to a competitor's new product release, adapting fast enough must be one of your strategic goals.

> *When outcomes are uncertain, answers hard to devise, that's the time to form a team, tap dreams, and improvise…. Putting lipstick on a bulldog won't transform enough. Makeup can't hide everything; change takes deeper stuff.[1]*

Adaptive Leadership

Leadership material—books, articles, blogs—is full of platitudes. "Learn from your mistakes" is a classic one. Has any leadership book published in the last 20 years not voiced this platitude? So, as Kanter says, let's attempt to go a little deeper. What are the things that make changing to an adaptive leadership culture so challenging?

1. Kanter, Rosabeth Moss. *e-Volve!: Succeeding in the Digital Culture of Tomorrow.* Boston: Harvard Business School Press, 2001.

"Agility is the ability to create and respond to change in order to succeed in an uncertain and turbulent environment."[2]

— Jim Highsmith

Let's start this journey with an example. In the early years of the agile movement, and in some organizations today, managers had to overcome a significant change in the timing of their discomfort. In the traditional process of upfront planning and specification, managers became "comfortable" that the project would succeed. "Surely with all this front-end work and detailed documentation, the project will go as planned," they said. However, as projects progressed, their comfort level often decreased as the team ran into problems. Near the project's planned ending, usually as tests began failing, their discomfort increased dramatically.

Agile introduced more discomfort at the beginning of projects, rather than at the end, by accepting the looming uncertainty of plans that were not prescribed in detail. There is always some discomfort toward the end—EDGE doesn't abandon Murphy's Law. On waterfall projects, however, the discomfort at the end tended to be at a panic level. On agile projects, comfort tended to increase over the life of the projects as uncertainties were dealt with and completed features delivered. You would think that this latter scenario would be more attractive to managers and leaders—but in one case it was a big change that proved difficult to overcome. A mid-level manager in a 1000-employee software company (a company making a transition to agile) made the comment, "The managers who commit to a plan, even one they absolutely know is unachievable, are rewarded. Those managers who question the plans, and admit to the uncertainty of the plan, are castigated for not getting 'with the program.' Even when the plan-supporting managers are proved wrong in the end, they get better performance reviews. Agreeing to poor plans that upper management 'wishes' were achievable wins out over realism."[3]

So, what is adaptive leadership? Several years ago Pat Reed and Jim Highsmith pioneered a class in adaptive leadership at the University of California at Berkeley. One diagram, filled with interlocking circles, had more than 30 topics to be covered in the class. Adaptive leadership—where do we

2. Highsmith, Jim. *Agile Software Development Ecosystems,* Boston: Pearson Education, 2002.
3. We have often referred to this as "wish-based planning."

start, where do we go, where do we finish? It's not a surprise that the content of adaptive leadership is so elusive—just think of all the books written about leadership in general in the last 25 years.

Remember the challenge you face—transforming to a digital business as exploding technology opportunities are transforming our world. The concepts that transformed the software world were contained in the Agile Manifesto, and those ideas can form the basis for defining the essence of adaptive leadership—people and their interactions, delivering actual products and services (code), adjusting and learning, and customer focus. The Agile Manifesto uses somewhat different words, but these four values form the essence of agile.

> A digital transformation is not a project with a beginning and an end. It is a continuous process.

True digital transformations involve a lot of change to fundamental ideas that organizations have operated on for a long time. Changing your fitness functions, embracing Tech@Core, moving from project to product thinking, and building autonomous teams are all in their own right big changes—much less trying to accomplish them together.

> *"Shortcomings in organizational culture are one of the main barriers to company success in the digital age. That is a central finding from McKinsey's recent survey of global executives, which highlighted three digital-culture deficiencies: functional and departmental silos, a fear of taking risks, and difficulty forming and acting on a single view of the customer."*
>
> —Julie Goran, Laura LaBerge, and Ramesh Srinivasan, "Culture for a Digital Age," *McKinsey Quarterly*, July 2017

Adaptive leaders must have the ability to articulate both core values and the competencies and practices that reflect those values. They must be bold in the changes they propose, and persistent in leading others through the morass that change entails. Put simply, you must *lead*. Lead in these four behavioral ways:

- Encourage an adaptive mindset.
- Lead change.

- Be bold.
- Inspire others.

Changing behavior takes courage, as in the courageous executive concept introduced in Chapter 1, The Big Picture. Without courageous leaders, no digital transformation will occur: There are just too many obstacles. Changing mindsets, leading change, being bold, inspiring others, and learning what works and what doesn't—all require overcoming the status quo, learning, and moving ahead.

Encourage an Adaptive Mindset

An adaptive mindset is one of Envision–Explore, rather than the traditional Plan–Do.

The Agile Manifesto is very explicit in its use of the word "over" rather than "versus" in describing preferred courses of action. The word "over" indicates that one item is more important than the other, not that the second item is unimportant. There are times and situations in which a Plan–Do mindset would be appropriate, but Envision–Explore will still be the primary mindset of an adaptive leader.

Envision–Explore could also be called Hypothesis–Experiment, although the latter doesn't roll off the tongue quite as smoothly. Envision speaks to possibility, externality with customers, value, outcome orientation, and blueprint orientation, whereas Explore speaks to openness to change, responsiveness, autonomy, and learning. Plan–Do brings to mind internal focus, output measures, reacting to threats, delegation, and detail task orientation.

> *"In a nutshell, senior executives must move the company—and themselves—away from outmoded command-and-control behaviors and structures that are ill-suited to today's rapid digital world."*
>
> —Oliver Bossert, Alena Kretzberg, and Jürgen Laartz, "Unleashing the Power of Small, Independent Teams," *McKinsey Quarterly*, July 2018

The use of the term "bet" in the Lean Value Tree (LVT) reinforces the idea of experimentation. Given a particular goal (which itself might change), you place "bets" on how best to achieve that goal. Some bets work out and deliver value, some need to be dropped, and others require significant modification (a pivot).

The legacy of decades of a Plan–Do culture is difficult to overcome. We are drawn to certainty, not ambiguity. Admitting "I don't know" has not been a path to managerial success, but more a path to ridicule. Adaptive leaders have to overcome this negative connotation associated with not knowing, by expressing it in another way: "I know our vision. I know we will experiment with how to get there and eventually succeed." Adaptive leaders help teams build confidence in their process and ability to solve difficult problems.

Plans have historically included schedules and costs. Adaptive leaders don't abandon these, but redefine them as constraints, not objectives. The constraints are real and affect how bets and initiatives are implemented. One reason short iterations are so critical to experimentation is that they force difficult decisions—early and often.

Envision–Explore defines an experimental process—one that iterates to a good solution. However, it can also oscillate back and forth without coming to a good solution. Without clear goals, exploration will be too open-ended and lead to endless investigations. The goals need to be broad enough so that explorations are useful, but narrow enough that they are achievable. Good measures of success help you bring the goals into greater focus and ensure that solutions deliver value. They also provide the team with the ability to determine if they are getting closer, or further away from the desired outcome. In other words, Measures of Success (MoS) are the compass for the EDGE steering mechanism.

Exploring is the process of delivering results—whether that is software, services, or other products. In the software business, the approach that epitomizes exploration is agile delivery. It focuses on speed, learning, and adjusting—just what experimentation requires. In today's world of exponentially expanding opportunities, ambiguity, and uncertainty, a culture of experimentation—guided experimentation, to be sure—needs to permeate your enterprise. Chapter 2, Tech@Core, addressed the technical components of experimentation. But even the best exploration tools are useless without leadership support and encouragement.

In the LVT, the second-level items are called bets. Agile teams talk about hypotheses and then testing those hypotheses. Replacing the word "plan" with "bet" or "speculate" recognizes that prescriptive plans no longer work in our era of uncertainty and change. Thinking of bets and initiatives as experiments helps overcome the stigma of plans. The first step is revising your planning and execution strategy.

> You can't plan away uncertainty; you need to experiment it away.

Lead Change

This book contains a number of concepts and practices critical to a digital transformation:

- Customer value fitness function
- Autonomous teams
- Product thinking
- Tech@Core
- Portfolio management using LVTs and MoS
- Collaborative decision making

All of these areas require change—change that needs to be led. The first order of business is to think about how each of these changes affect you. As a leader, some of these changes may come easier than others. While some may sound easy, they may be very difficult in practice. For example, changing your fitness function may sound easy; after all, who could be opposed to focusing on customer value? Nevertheless, making the change requires changing decades of buildup of practices, processes, personal beliefs, and performance measures.

One of the changes you as an adaptive leader need to support and guide is the transition to autonomous teams. Authors have been writing about teamwork and team dynamics for decades. *The Wisdom of Teams* by Jon Katzenbach and Douglas K. Smith,[4] originally published in 1993, reignited

---

4. Katzenbach, Jon R., and Douglas K. Smith. *The Wisdom of Teams: Creating the High-Performance Organization*. Reprint edition. Boston: Harvard Business Review Press, 2015.

interest in teams and how to make them effective. Agile proponents have championed a blend of high-performance, self-sufficient, empowered, autonomous teams since the inclusion of the value "people and interactions over process and tools" in the Agile Manifesto. Autonomy is one of the three principal motivators, according to Daniel Pink. But like the other changes required to become an adaptive leader, creating autonomous teams, figuring out their goals and boundaries, and helping them grow into high-performance teams are difficult. When teams are granted more power, leaders inevitably have less. It can be a difficult transition.

Manage Anxiety

One of the most difficult roles in leading change is that of empathetic listener. You are undertaking a digital transformation because of economic forces of change—external pressure. Making this transition requires multiple changes to processes, organization, and culture—internal pressure. Once again, leaders need to balance on the edge: They must acknowledge their own and their staff's anxiety without multiplying it, but not be complacent and ignore it.

Managing Anxiety

In the early 2000s, Jim worked with a Canadian firm that was developing cell phone operating system software. During this early market phase for cell phones, requirements from phone companies were constantly evolving, as were industry standards. Software developers at this company were in a constant state of flux and anxiety.

Unfortunately, several of the first-line leaders magnified that anxiety. To staff comments like "Things are really messed up," these leaders, who were also anxious, would respond, "They sure are." Their response intensified the anxiety. Chief among the complaints were constantly changing requirements. The staff's "solution" was to freeze requirements, thereby reducing anxiety. However, as Jim pointed out, freezing requirements would make the company noncompetitive in the market.

Instead of concurring with the "messed up" comment, the recommendation was that the leaders acknowledge the anxiety, but also remind staff that turmoil was the natural state in this market. Their job was to develop practices that would enable the company to respond to market conditions better than its competitors, but not to succumb to change by ignoring it.

One morning a few weeks later, the staff walked into the office and found balloons flying all around. One of the managers announced, "We are celebrating anxiety," which, as intended, helped the teams reduce their level of anxiety.

Nearly every aspect of adaptive leadership requires balancing. You need to express confidence in the future, yet not ignore the reality of the present. Teams need to think positively about their vision and desired outcomes, yet remain open to data that indicates the need to pivot the solution. As an adaptive leader, you must learn to balance anxiety and progress.

Overcoming the Culture of Fear

One of the biggest barriers to experimentation and learning is overcoming the culture of fear.

A recent Google study[5] investigated what high-performing teams had in common. The most important trait? Psychological safety. That means team members share the belief that they won't be punished when they make a mistake. Encouraging positive emotions during the creative process broadens this mindset. Barbara Fredrickson[6] found that having such a mindset enables the brain to discover new knowledge and skills, thereby building new resources to tackle problems. Leaders who create a safe environment foster more open-minded, creative, and resilient team members. Incubating

5. Rozovsky, Julia. "The Five Keys to a Successful Google Team." *re:Work*, November 17, 2015. https://rework.withgoogle.com/blog/five-keys-to-a-successful-google-team/.
6. Fredrickson, Barbara L. "Updated Thinking on Positivity Ratios." *American Psychologist* 68, no. 9 (December 1, 2013).

this mindset at scale creates a learning culture that can sense and respond to the changing environment.

"Courage is not the absence of fear, but rather the judgement that something else is more important than the fear."[7]

—David Robinson

Building your practice of experimentation includes overcoming a culture of fear that is often couched as fear of failure, but is actually much more. While we can talk about fear of failure, fear of power loss, or fear of job loss, at the core of these lies the fear of loss of respect. The fear of loss of respect—especially that of peers—derails many teams.

The technology arena is to a great extent a meritocracy, which can be both good and bad. Expertise is critical to executing on your bets and initiatives, but experts can cause conflict on self-sufficient teams because maintaining respect across different experts can be difficult. All too often, the undercurrent is illustrated by unspoken but understood thoughts: "If you don't understand my area of expertise, then you don't deserve respect."

Meritocracy, creativity, diversity, and respect—the interplay of these four concepts drives experimentation success. First, you need expertise because of the complexity of the technology (for example, the software technology "stack" is exponentially more complex than it was just 10 years ago). Second, you need multiple forms of diversity—multiple technology experts, business and technical skills, and social diversity (gender, ethnicity, geographic, and more). The wider your diversity, the wider your potential creativity—unless that same diversity keeps the team from jelling. Often respect is limited to "my" group, often one that is narrowly defined by a particular skill. From a technical perspective, you might think of developers and business analysts: There may be respect within each of those groups but limited respect across them. Or, think about engineering and marketing: Often these specialties don't respect each other's expertise.

An experimentation mindset admits that we don't have the right answer and that we have a difficult problem to solve, one that needs creativity and diversity. Two things help us overcome the fear that experimentation often

---

7. Robinson, David. "Courage—Critical Success Factor for Innovation." Blog post, October 4, 2014. http://www.false-summits.com/?cat=20.

breeds—respect and trust. Respect relates to expertise, and trust to execution. "I *respect* your abilities to help this team. I *trust* you to accomplish what you agreed to do." Self-sufficient teams have the advantage of learning about others' abilities, and that increases respect.

> **Note**
>
> Jim was once the VP of sales and marketing for a small startup company. "I was fairly new in the job and recall sitting in a conference room with a cadre of potential client technical managers and lawyers from a large West Coast company. Running through my mind was my CEO's last comments to me that if I didn't get this contract signed we wouldn't make payroll next month. It gave me greater respect for sales people. Understanding this nail-biting part of the sales job was an eye opener."

The Thin-Slice Change Strategy

The topic of change management is much too broad to cover thoroughly in this book. There are many approaches to change management, as outlined in a raft of books. We don't want this book to turn into a change management book, so our recommendation to you is simple: Investigate different approaches, find one that appears to fit with your goals and culture, and use it!

Here, we will address just a small, but important piece of change management as it applies to digital transformation—namely, your coverage strategy. That is, how do you apply change that includes technology to your organization: all in, incremental (either top-down or bottom-up), or thin slice? In the early days of agile development, almost all implementations were bottom-up. A team or two was given the OK to try this "agile" stuff (or they sneaked it in without an OK). If they proved successful, other teams might try it, and over time a number of teams implemented this newfangled approach. Typically the use grew slowly, and mainly within software development teams (often without testing or product management involvement). Often these teams were labeled as "rogue" and given little organizational support. Expansion upward into project management or IT management ranks was usually slow, or nonexistent.

Rogue Teams Implemented Agile

A speaker at an early agile conference got this question from the audience: "How do you get your manager to approve refactoring (an agile technical practice) time?" "Well," said the speaker, "Just do it. Refactoring is a practice that every developer should be using. Besides, how would your manager know if you are factoring or refactoring!"

As agile became more widely used, a few organizations—typically software companies—tried top-down implementations in which senior executives decreed that all teams would use agile. The success of these decrees was variable, but often less successful than the bottom-up approaches. In the 1980s and 1990s, many, if not most, traditional waterfall methodology implementations were top-down. These implementations failed because they offered nothing to development teams except extra paperwork and bureaucracy.

Top-Down Failure

Back when waterfall methodologies were in vogue, one large telecommunications company tried three software engineering methodologies over a period of five to six years. These were all installed in a top-down manner with little input from developers, testers, and others at the staff level who were trying to implement software. The bureaucratic processes and documentation were a burden on getting the job done, not a help. Agile success was often achieved through a bottom-up effort. It's clear that it's not just the strategy that matters, but also the philosophy behind the strategy.

Both top-down and bottom-up implementations could be incremental or all-in approaches—changing a team or two at a time versus trying to change everyone, from teams to management, at once. All the various combinations and permutations of these change strategies succeeded, but also often failed. At an agile conference several years ago, Jim was talking with a

VP from a very large Chinese company. "How many agile projects did you do this year?" Jim inquired. "Six" was the response. "How many would you like to do next year?" was the next question. "About 200" was the response. "What do you think the probability of going top-down from 6 to 200 agile teams in a year is?" (You can make your own guess.)

In a top-down approach, organizational support and infrastructure may be easier to obtain, but actual use by delivery teams goes slowly. A bottom-up strategy generates the opposite result—more use at the team level but challenges getting management support and process and infrastructure changes.

If your goal is to transform an entire organization, the strategy we've found most successful is a "thin slice" implementation. The strategy is not to change an entire organization at one time, but to change all levels, from development team to senior management, for one to a few delivery initiatives. In the bottom-up era, many efforts were confined to developers. Particularly with bottom-up implementations, management tends to grant exceptions to policies, procedures, and other infrastructure items but doesn't engage in actually changing them. In a thin-slice approach, teams have much broader functional participation—developers, technical specialists, testers, operations, and product and project management. In addition, managers and executives in both the IT and business hierarchy participate. By using this thin-slice approach, the organization learns from successes and challenges very quickly.

Being fractal is one of the characteristics of EDGE. Fractals are patterns that are repeated at multiple levels. For example, the LVT is fractal in that similar activities happen at each level—goal, bet, and initiative. The thin-slice practice is also fractal. It was first introduced in Chapter 6, Building a Product Mindset, as a way of breaking down products into smaller chunks of business functionality that "sliced" along lines of customer value and included all the technology components needed to implement the slice. Using a thin-slice strategy for organizational development is similar in that the slice includes all levels of an organization that support a delivery team.

At an organizational level, this thin-slice approach is similar to the agile approach to software development—planning and executing business "stories" rather than developing by technical layers. The technical layer approach had one group doing the user interface, another doing the business logic, another doing database development, and yet another handling testing. Customer value was often the last thing these groups thought about: They just built their individual components. As you might guess, integrating these pieces was often a nightmare. The story approach focuses on an increment of business functionality—delivering something useful and understandable—to the customer.

In *Secrets of Consulting*, author Jerry Weinberg states, "Never promise more than 10% improvement."[8] Change is always more difficult than you planned for. The optimal approach to change involves all levels of management and delivery teams at the same time—but limited in the breadth of impact. Having a few teams (one to three) at the delivery level (including product managers/owners, developers, testers, operations staff, and other necessary personnel) learning a new approach (agile) while management is addressing infrastructure items for these teams (policies, accounting practices, governance, performance measurements, and staffing) enables the organization to learn what works and what doesn't at multiple levels—quickly. The next product (or project) builds on that learning when undertaking the next slice. As slices accumulate, more and more of the organization—at all levels—participates.

With any significant change, organizational "antibodies" will likely appear. Like biological antibodies, they are resistant to change and try to move back toward the status quo. This is a particular issue with bottom-up change, as middle managers often take on the antibody mantle. Because the focus of change is on delivery teams, few managers are engaged for a long time period, giving them time to hone their anti-change rationale. Antibodies are illustrative of the problems of scaling change whether you use a thin-slice strategy or another approach. But resistance can also be a source of learning.

What Not to Change

Much of this chapter, and the book as a whole, is about change, about adapting. However, the world of opportunities and your potential response

---

8. Weinberg, Gerald M. *The Secrets of Consulting*. New York: Dorset House Publishing, 1985.

to those opportunities, is infinite. As an adaptive leader, you need to understand when to change and when not to. You can build an understanding of when not to change by thinking separately about core values that don't change and operating practices and specific goals and strategies that do.

For software development, the Agile Manifesto's four value statements have guided practitioners for nearly 20 years (as of the release of this book). While some have proposed additions or modifications to the value statements, they have remained core to the success of the agile movement. There are very few aspects of software engineering, or general management for that matter, that are still at the forefront of those disciples after 20 years. It speaks to the resilience of the agile movement that its core values have stood the test of time. But there have also been changes. As agile practices have approached mainstream status, organizations have molded practices and processes to their own unique situations, and strategies for expanding agile into wider organizations uses have all been accomplished—guided by four short, concise value statements.

Your next level of what not to change is the LVT. While many view the LVT as a guide to what to do, a well-articulated LVT can also help us determine *what not to do*. "Does this help us meet goal 1?" would be a useful type of question to keep in mind. The universe of things you could do is vast compared to the number of things you should do. So part of succeeding at adapting fast enough is being good at knowing when to change and when not to.

Be Bold

A digital transformation requires leaders with a well-articulated purpose that inspires those around them. It is driven by an experimental process and a technology platform geared toward experimentation, but in the end people and culture dictate success. This transformation doesn't happen unless you have executives and leaders who have the courage to be bold and champion bold investments.

Earlier in this book, we introduced the biological concept of fitness function. In biological evolution, mutations provide the mechanism for adaptation: Good mutations further the organism's fitness goals, whereas bad mutations die out. The mutation mechanism has both an upside and a downside. The upside is that organisms can adapt to changes in the ecosystem. The downside is that they take time, sometimes tens of thousands of years. When the environment changes quickly—think of the meteor impact that cooled the earth rapidly about 65 million years ago and led to the demise of dinosaurs—your ability to adapt can be severely challenged. Of course, the extinction of the dinosaurs also aided the evolution of mammals.

Businesses don't have thousands of years to adapt, and often not even tens of years. However, businesses do need a mechanism similar to mutations that can act as a catalyst for adaptation to environmental changes. The business mechanism is guided experimentation. Random experimentation might work—eventually—but you don't have "eventually": You need to adapt *now*.

The first guide to your experimentation is your LVT. It provides goals and boundaries. Bold experimentation doesn't end with the product: Your guided experiments could cover organizational structure, business model, a technology platform, and culture. The outcomes, measured by your choice of MoS, also help bound experimentation.

During the first week of the 2018 Winter Olympics was the qualification round for men's snowboard half-pipe. Scores kept escalating—91, 93, 95. This was an unprecedented number of scores in the 90s. American two-time gold medal winner Shaun White went last. Since it was just a qualifying round, he only had to score in the top 12 to move on. But he chose to go big, to go bold—and put up the highest score of the day, 98.5. In the finals, on the last run as the last shredder down the pipe, White faced a daunting score of 95 from the previous competitor. Once again, his boldness and competitive spirit won the day: He scored 97.75. Boldness, striving to be the best, will sustain teams and individuals through the difficulties of transformation. Boldness and courage are needed for sustained innovation—and, of course, a team with the right capabilities.

Leading a digital transformation can be a daunting task, in large measure because it affects financial and power relationships in an organization. When you read about or have a consultant tell you about a process such as EDGE, it appears that there is a direct cause and effect. Build an LVT, define MoS, prioritize initiatives, and then you get results. The piece that is often missed is that success and failure are more about judgment and experience than about process. Remember again the agile value of "people and interactions over process and tools." The culture of individuals and their collaboration are key to success.

Who Invented the Digital Camera?

In the mid-1970s, a young newly hired engineer, Steven Sasson, invented the digital camera while working for Kodak. As he tried to sell the digital camera idea inside Kodak, he ran up against obstacles. "The main objections came from the marketing and business sides. Kodak had a virtual monopoly on the United States photography market, and made money on every step of the photographic process."[9]

Just imagine an executive investment committee meeting. The senior VP of the film market says, "We need $50 million to invest in extending our film market. The return on investment is 30%, the payback is 12 months, and it will solidify us as the number 1 company in film and film cameras." Then the manager of the fledgling digital camera department gets up and says, "We need $50 million to invest in breaking into this new and potentially lucrative market. We can't really estimate the return on investment and the payback might be three to five years." Who do you think gets the money? When did the film market go belly up and bankrupt Kodak, which was for many years a very large and respected enterprise? That said, it's easy to look back and see what you should have done. But how do you look into the future, and invest wisely in it?

Of course, you should also think about what the future brought to the digital camera business. In a short period of time, the low- and mid-range digital camera business was severely impacted by cameras in smartphones. This required a serious pivot in a new business that was just getting started.

9. Estrin, James. "Kodak's First Digital Moment." *The New York Times*, August 12, 2015.

Riding Paradox

What is an adaptive leader or manager? There are countless answers to this question revolving around the desirable characteristics, mindset, or behaviors—for example, collaborative, light touch, servant, and failure tolerant. One of the critical traits is that of "and" rather than "or" leadership. The most pressing issues to face leaders are usually paradoxical; they appear to have contradictory solutions. Consider, for example, the paradox of needing predictable delivery while also needing to be flexible and adapt over the life of a project. Agile teams face difficult choices because managers haven't addressed this paradox. They often continue to admonish teams to do both, without really giving them direction about how. Alternatively, they may give lip service to adaptability and focus on delivering to plan—scope, schedule, and cost—just like in the waterfall development days. Or worse, they may focus on velocity and forget quality.

Agile teams succeed, in part, because they embrace seeing reality, the reality that "stuff" happens during a project and that the path to success involves adaptation. Ambiguity, risk, and uncertainty are an integral part of innovative projects today. As such, they offer leaders paradoxical situations—situations that require backing away from the direct paradox and figuring out inclusive solutions. Adaptive leaders need to become "riders of paradox."[10]

Agile leaders need the courage to view issues from different perspectives, to gather data without undue prejudice, to formulate both/and rather than either/or resolutions. Too few organizations make it past what we have labeled "prescriptive agility," which should be an oxymoron, but unfortunately isn't. These organizations are as rigid about their agile implementations as they were previously about their heavy methodologies! They fail to move beyond rules to understanding. Adaptive leaders need to be riders of paradox, always thinking, "how can I do this AND that" at the same time.

> *"Learn the law very well, so you will know how to disobey it properly."*
>
> —The Dalai Lama

10. This section is excerpted from Highsmith, Jim. *Adaptive Leadership*: *Accelerating Enterprise Agility*. Boston: Addison-Wesley, 2013.

We will illustrate with two other examples from software development, issues that have been written about as either/or cases: waterfall versus agile, and BUFD (big upfront design) versus NUFD (no upfront design). In each case, proponents on either side have set the other up as an enemy to be defeated, rather than considering what is useful in each approach. The bottom line is that all models are flawed, but all are also potentially useful. The true adaptive leader—whether an iteration manager, a project manager, a technical lead, a development vice president, or a CIO—attempts to "include" the best from different models. It's easy to be an "or" leader. Pick a side and state your case loudly, over and over again, until the opposition gives up. It's much more difficult to be an "and" leader, balancing between seemingly opposite strategies. However, in our ever-changing and turbulent world, slavishly following the "one right answer" is a recipe for disaster.

We live in a culture of absolutes—think of the current rhetoric of our political parties—but most people recognize that reality imposes a lot of gray. If we think human (or business) affairs are rational, then we attack everything as a problem to be solved by highlighting the issue, gathering facts, looking for root causes, formulating solutions, and implementing the solution. Once we're done, it's "problem solved" and on to the next problem.

But what astute managers have learned is that most serious issues are not problems, but rather paradoxes that arise again and again. Paradoxes aren't solved once and for all; they require balancing actions again and again. There is even difficulty finding a word for the outcome of a paradox. A "problem" has a solution, but what is the outcome of a paradox—a "temporary solution"? The best word seems to be "resolution," which has a dynamic aspect to it that "solution" doesn't. So, problems have solutions whereas paradoxes have resolutions.

Take, for example, the issue of short-term versus long-term focus. There isn't a single answer to this issue; a balancing needs to occur from one time frame to another. When a company is in serious financial trouble, working on a five-year strategic plan probably isn't a good use of management time.

The ability to differentiate between problems and paradoxes, along with the ability to balance paradoxical resolutions time after time, are among the defining characteristics of an adaptive leader. These abilities don't come easily because discernment and judgment are involved. Paradoxes that leaders face include the following:

- Accountability versus autonomy
- Hierarchical control versus self-organization
- Predictability versus adaptability
- Efficiency versus responsiveness

None of these is a problem, and none has an easy solution. Any resolution must contain elements of both—delicate balancing acts that change over time. Take the issue of predictability versus adaptability. The traditional mandate that "We must be within 5 percent (or whatever number) of our schedule or cost plan" just doesn't drive people in the right direction if we want them to learn and adapt over time. Conversely, not giving any predictions doesn't work either. Acknowledging a paradox means giving up the notion that you are in control and can dictate (plan) the future. At the same time, you cannot take a totally cavalier "let's wait and see what happens" approach. Living with paradoxes means planning, but not becoming wedded to the plan. It means sensing when actual events override the plan and responding with the appropriate "resolution." Learning to do this well is a keystone of adaptive leadership.

Inspire Others

Adaptive leadership is about leading. It's about defining and embracing an ambitious vision. It's about having the courage to push through negativism. It's about having the grit to persist in the hard work required to change. It's about persistence—the willingness to adjust and move forward, but not giving up on the vision.

Motivation has gotten a bad rap in recent years as academics and consultants have moved on to "modern" concepts. While motivation means the willingness or desire to do something, it has often been considered manipulative. But studies indicate that large percentages of employees are not engaged in their work. They work, but are not inspired to fully engage.[11]

11. Kruse, Kevin. "Why Employee Engagement? (These 28 Research Studies Prove the Benefits)," *Forbes*, 2012. https://www.forbes.com/sites/kevinkruse/2012/09/04/why-employee-engagement/#4fdcfb303aab.

Transformations are hard and scary; so is innovation. Both of these create emotional roller coasters for staff and leaders. Leaders must articulate the vision, in multiple different ways, to encourage engagement.

While inspiration, courage, persistence, and engagement are important traits, they sometimes sound academic. That is why we are drawn to the concept of "grit." The first time Linda tried a new recipe using Australia's venerable Vegemite, her dog wouldn't even touch it. He didn't fancy the next six versions, either. Rather than turn in her chef apron, Linda researched tried-and-tested flavor pairings, which inspired her to make Vegemite lamb shanks. Delicious!

> *"Gritty teams collectively have the same traits that gritty individuals do: a desire to work hard, learn, and improve; resilience in the face of setbacks; and a strong sense of priorities and purpose."*[12]

Organizational grit is the perseverance to continuously learn from set backs so that it becomes "just the way we do things around here." It's about a commitment to solving a problem incorporating feedback, experimentation, and learnings from failures. Customers didn't like the first prototype? Product pitch didn't make it past the funding round with stakeholders? That's not the end of the world in a company with strong organizational grit. Employees take the learnings and find better ways to solve the same problem. In such organizations, teams are rewarded for learning, not punished for failing.

Grit refers to strength of character and the resolve to get something done—no matter what. The most famous story of grit comes from the 1969 movie *True Grit*, for which actor John Wayne won his only Academy Award. Wayne's character Rooster Cogburn persisted in the face of multiple setbacks and his own limitations (he is a falling-down drunk at the beginning of the movie) to eventually get the bad guys.

12. Lee, Thomas H., and Angela L. Duckworth. "Organizational Grit." *Harvard Business Review*, September–October 2018.

Final Thoughts

In many ways, management is about the present whereas leadership is about the future—a future of adapting to change. Adapting is about uncertainty, anxiety, experimenting, judgment, fear, innovation, collaboration, and decision making. It is about envisioning and exploring, rather than planning and doing. It is about bold, gritty leadership and inspiring others to engage in the future.

Adaptive leadership is a critical component of the EDGE operating model. Take a new style of leadership away from your transformation and it's unlikely to end well. However, the same can be said for other components, such as Tech@Core or building an LVT. While every organization needs to adapt the components of EDGE to its own situation, don't forget that you have to understand how the components are integrated to form a whole. Don't leave out a key piece.

Chapter 11

EDGE: Exploring Your Transformative Future

You've seen the "hockey sticks" in every book on change. Whether they represent population growth, microchip density driven by Moore's Law, or the shrinking of polar glacial ice, hockey stick curves indicate the accelerating pace of change. But big change events have been around for a long time. Less known than the extinction event surrounding the disappearance of the dinosaurs was the more catastrophic late Permian event, 225 million years ago, when 96 percent of all living species vanished from earth.[1] Hundreds of species, many superbly honed as the fittest in their environment, died in the Permian extinction. Some, barely surviving in small Permian ecological niches, accidentally happened to have characteristics allowing them to flourish in the subsequent Triassic period. The bigger the change, particularly in the external environment (markets, technology, economy), the larger the chance of failure—it might be survival of the luckiest.

Are we living through a Permian extinction for businesses and other organizations? Can we improve on the survival of the luckiest? Darwin and other evolutionary biologists give us a survival of the fittest strategy, and many say the key fitness capability is adaptability. Another group of

---

1. Gould, Stephen Jay. *Wonderful Life: The Burgess Shale and the Nature of History.* New York: W. W. Norton and Company, 1989.

biologists, led by John Holland,[2] postulate that survival of the fittest isn't powerful enough and that *arrival of the fittest*— that is, cooperation and collaboration rather than competition—is more important. Do these biological analogies extend into the business world?

An organization's answer to the question *how can we adapt fast enough* may mean the difference between thriving in the future economy (which starts tomorrow) and going the way of buggy whip companies or bricks-and-mortar bookstores. It isn't an easy question to answer. Who do you need to be faster than? How many hotel chains anticipated Airbnb? Who anticipated the sharing economy that Airbnb epitomized? How did hotel chains respond? How do you stay in business while you adapt?

Take the example of JC Penney. Several years ago, the firm brought in a new CEO from Apple's retail operation who tried to remake the company. The changes were devastating to sales and profitability, and the company turned to previous executives to right the ship. But the entire retail market is in a state of confusion and uncertainty. The real question for JC Penney and many others remains: Which business model means success in the long term? Maybe the revised model was the correct one for the future but the transition cost was just too high. Time will tell if going back to the traditional model just bought the retailer a few more years or will bring a bright future. Was the company too slow to adapt in the beginning or too fast to discard the model changes? Your digital transformation timing will be important because your business model will change as well. Being late and operating in a catch-up mode to competitors is an uncomfortable place to be, as many enterprises are learning, but being too early and losing existing customers before your new strategy kicks in can be just as uncomfortable. However, becoming something different and being uncomfortable go hand-in-hand.

Leading into your future first requires that you turn a vast sea of opportunities into targeted goals that support your organization's purpose and vision. We will assume that because you are here and have read most of this book by now, your vision involves becoming a digital enterprise. To become an Envision–Explore rather than a Plan–Do organization, you need to think about how you measure success—your high-level fitness function.

2. Holland, John H. *Hidden Order: How Adaptation Builds Complexity*. Reading, MA: Addison-Wesley, 1995.

Return on investment (ROI) is now a necessary, but insufficient, Measure of Success (MoS). Customer value, even though it is more difficult to measure, measures success in a way that encourages the changes needed.

The Lean Value Tree (LVT) embodies the process of breaking the vision into goals, bets, and initiatives. At every level, some opportunities are refined into more detail while others are discarded. Critical to this refinement is coming up with good MoS, focusing on customer outcomes—things that provide value to your customers.

However, coming up with a well-populated LVT is only half the process. Concurrently with developing the LVT, you need to understand the capabilities required to achieve those goals and realistically assess yours, including how you can acquire capabilities that are lacking. We should point out here that technology provides both opportunities to be analyzed and capabilities to implement goals. We have found that a realistic assessment of capabilities is often one of the most difficult tasks.

Think of a metaphor from another endeavor—mountaineering. Is your goal to do a strenuous climb (basically a hike) up a moderate Colorado fourteener,[3] or do you want to climb one of the most dangerous mountains in the world, K2?[4] Generally, people know something about Mount Everest and the dangers there, as the press has reported on a series of fatalities in the last several decades.[5] K2 is much more challenging and dangerous. Think about the capabilities needed to hike a fourteener versus K2—from physical conditioning, to climbing skills, to planning and logistics, to mental toughness, to risk assessment. Executing business goals is no different: There are K2-like goals and fourteener-like goals, and it's best not to get them mixed up. Many climbing teams have the endurance and skills to ascend that moderate fourteener; few highly skilled and fit teams have succeeded on K2. Matching goals and capabilities isn't as straightforward as it might seem.

3. In Colorado, there are 53 peaks more than 14,000 feet in elevation that are referred to as fourteeners.
4. At 28,251 feet elevation, K2 (referred to as the Savage Mountain) is the second highest mountain in the world (after Mount Everest) and has the second highest fatality rate for climbers (after Annapurna).
5. Krakauer, Jon. *Into Thin Air: A Personal Account of the Mt. Everest Disaster.* New York: Villard Books, 1997.

While working on the LVT and MoS, the product people on the team and within the product organization are concurrently developing product blueprints to ensure that over the longer term the team, management, and customers have an understanding of how you intend to evolve your products. Organizational structures will also change as businesses morph from functional hierarchies to product-oriented autonomous teams.

Technology provides two potential benefits. On the one hand, the advances in technology create product and service opportunities; on the other hand, technology provides new capabilities to build those products. That raises a set of questions for everyone—executives, leaders, technologists. How can you understand social media if you have never used Facebook, Twitter, or Instagram? Can you visualize how virtual reality might be as big a jump in computer interface design as the jump from nongraphical to graphical interfaces? Do you know how big data analysis might help you better understand customers? It's not enough for executives and others to fund technology, you must *understand* technology! That leads to one of our keys to digital transformation—embracing Tech@Core.

Tech@Core, LVT, MoS, and product blueprints are all involved in turning nebulous opportunities into focused plans. Analyzing the capabilities needed to implement those plans follows. But both of these—opportunities and capabilities—require leadership, organization, and governance.

As we make the jump to the Fourth Industrial Revolution driven by the technology, we have to change how we work together. Creativity and innovation needed are more likely to bubble up than to bubble down. Diverse customer needs and diverse technology components require equally diverse teams, at every level of your organization, who can collaborate, make good decisions, learn and adapt, and deliver customer value. Organizations themselves need to be reorganized along value-chain links rather than traditional functional hierarchies. Teams need to be both self-sufficient and autonomous.

You need to tear executives and managers away from their comfort zone. You need to adapt, but not oscillate. You need to establish a clear and consistent vision and adaptive culture, providing your organization with a common core of principles that persists and concurrently a mindset that learns and adapts to evolving conditions. You need to persist and know when not to persist. You need to give up the notion of always being in control and the bureaucracy that inevitably builds up to ensure control. You need just enough governance—a level that is effective, but lightweight.

Accelerating change demands innovation in how we adapt fast enough. It requires more than faster product development: It demands radical changes in how we work together and how we invest in the future. To adapt fast enough, we have to move beyond scaling to infusing a different mindset throughout our organizations. Innovation and adaptation happen at the edge where structure meets chaos—where we all feel uncomfortable but excited. Balancing at the edge of chaos—keeping just enough structure to avoid debilitating chaos, while maintaining the freedom to spark innovation—isn't easy. A former CEO of ThoughtWorks once remarked, "We had eight key initiatives going into the year. It's now May and we eliminated three of the initiatives and added two more. I don't know if we are being adaptive or are just poor planners."

Have we gone too far in recommending so many changes in this book? Maybe. The different aspects of EDGE include focusing on customer value and speed and adaptability as fitness functions, addressing both opportunity and capability, understanding and applying EDGE principles, using the LVT and outcome-oriented MoS, adopting a product mindset, building autonomous teams, becoming adaptive leaders, and utilizing a lightweight governance model. The combination of these components defines an agile operating model that will assist you in transforming your organization into a digital enterprise that has a greater ability to adapt not only more quickly, but more effectively. As we said in the beginning, every organization is different and should decide to implement different aspects of EDGE—implement faster or slower, implement to different depths. But if your goal is to become a digital enterprise and to thrive in this rapidly changing and uncertain environment, you shouldn't underestimate the changes you need to make.

As we said at the beginning of Chapter 1, The Big Picture, EDGE is more about transforming than transformation. The path from the Industrial Age to the Digital Age can be long and winding. New technologies will arise. Both opportunities and competition will change. Ultimately, EDGE is more about the journey, the becoming, than the destination. So don't forget that transforming your enterprise will be hastened by concentrating on evolving your adaptive culture as you move toward that destination.

Index

facilitators for, 181
openness to ideas, 180–181
self-sufficient knowledge,
  177–178
slow decision making, 181–182
trust and respect, 179–180
willingness to participate,
  182–183
defect repairs, 126, 134
defining product, 106–107
delaying detail, 137
delegation, 160
delivery teams, 174
demand shaping, 136–137
digital enterprises, defined, 2
digital technology platforms
  asset ecosystems, 42–44
  defined, 38–40
  experimentation, 44–45
  friction reduction, 40–42
direct priority assignment, 140
direct value assignment, 140
discovery workshops, 104
diverse perspectives, 179

E

EDGE
  defined, 3
  operating model, 4, 5–7
  principles of, 49–57
    adaptive leadership, 54
    autonomous teams, 55–56
    collaborative decision making,
      57
    lightweight planning and
      governance, 53

outcome-based strategy, 51–52
value-based prioritization, 52–53
teams in, 169–170
edge of chaos, 3, 162, 215
elevator pitches, 107
empowerment, 160–161
Envision-Explore mindset, 19,
  192–194, 212–213
escalation processes, 141–142
executive teams, 173–174
experimentation
  boldness in, 202–204
  requirements for, 44–45

F

facilitators, 181
fitness function, 11–16, 28
fractals, 200
friction reduction, 40–42
funding allocation in Lean Value Tree
  (LVT), 71–72

G

geographic/market area categorization,
  76
goal teams, 173–174
goals
  adding new, 69
  defined, 63
  strategic portfolio ownership and,
    66–68
governance
  lightweight, 53, 145–155
    establishing, 146–151

strategy and, 61–62

terminology, 62

legacy systems. *See also* Business As
Usual (BAU)

defect repairs, 126

investment decisions for, 38

small enhancements, 125–126

technical debt from, 35–37, 127

lightweight planning and governance,
53, 145–155

establishing, 146–151

Periodic Value Reviews (PVR),
149–152, 155

rebalancing portfolio, 152–154

LVT. *See* Lean Value Tree (LVT)

M

Measures of Success (MoS), 79–85,
141

activity measures, 81

for Business as Usual (BAU), 127

business benefits, 81

customer value, 80–81

importance of, 79–80

leading and lagging measures,
82–83

number of, 83–84

portfolio differentiation, 84–85

Minimum Viable Product (MVP),
113–114

Moore, Geoffrey, 21

N

next-generation operating models,
building, 5

O

openness to ideas, 180–181

organizational alignment to business
capabilities, 183–186

organizational responsiveness,
9–10

outcome-based strategy, 51–52

P

paradoxes in leadership, 205–207

Periodic Value Reviews (PVR),
149–152, 155

Plan-Do mindset, 19, 192–194,
212–213

platforms

defined, 38

types of, 39–40

portfolio teams, 172–174

portfolios. *See* value-driven portfolios

principles

of EDGE, 49–57

adaptive leadership, 54

autonomous teams, 55–56

collaborative decision making,
57

lightweight planning and
governance, 53

outcome-based strategy, 51–52

value-based prioritization,
52–53

importance of, 49–50

prioritization. *See* value-based
prioritization

product blueprints, 214

defining product, 106–107

elements of, 107–110

Agile Development
Books, eBooks & Video

Whether are you a programmer, developer, or project manager InformIT has the most comprehensive collection of agile books, eBooks, and video training from the top thought leaders.

- Introductions & General Scrum Guides
- Culture, Leadership & Teams
- Development Practices
- Enterprise
- Product & Project Management
- Testing
- Requirements
- Video Short Courses

Visit **informit.com/agilecenter** to read sample chapters, shop, and watch video lessons from featured products.

Photo by izusek/gettyimages

Register Your Product at informit.com/register

Access additional benefits and **save 35%** on your next purchase

- Automatically receive a coupon for 35% off your next purchase, valid for 30 days. Look for your code in your InformIT cart or the Manage Codes section of your account page.

- Download available product updates.

- Access bonus material if available.*

- Check the box to hear from us and receive exclusive offers on new editions and related products.

*Registration benefits vary by product. Benefits will be listed on your account page under Registered Products.

InformIT.com—The Trusted Technology Learning Source

InformIT is the online home of information technology brands at Pearson, the world's foremost education company. At InformIT.com, you can:

- Shop our books, eBooks, software, and video training
- Take advantage of our special offers and promotions (informit.com/promotions)
- Sign up for special offers and content newsletter (informit.com/newsletters)
- Access thousands of free chapters and video lessons

Connect with InformIT—Visit informit.com/community

the trusted technology learning source

Addison-Wesley • Adobe Press • Cisco Press • Microsoft Press • Pearson IT Certification • Que • Sams • Peachpit Press

 Pearson